Lost Foundation:
A conversation with
18th century economist
Richard Cantillon

By Rand McGreal

For Shannon Austin,

A gift to my caring daughter, so she might instill economic wisdom in the minds of her three lovely daughters, Tatum, Aleah, and Everly.

Acknowledgement

I want to thank my main editor Joel Palmer for his thorough review and thoughtful guidance. I also want to thank Alan Rinzler for his insights and overall guidance. Although their help is greatly appreciated, the final form and content of this book originated in my own mind.

Table of Contents

Preface

A couple of years ago I discovered a remarkable economic construct that I thought could lift millions of people out of poverty, and wrote about it in *Rule of Money*. The book got little attention. Then a year ago I read Richard Cantillon's 18th century economics book, the *Essai*. Gradually, the pieces of a new economic vision came together for me. I realized my *Rule of Money* had been a natural extension of Cantillon's work. The problem I now faced was: how to communicate the new economic process I envisioned to enough people to turn over the political engine?

I knew the best approach would be for you and I to sit down with Richard Cantillon in front of a cracking fireplace and discuss how to implement this change. Since that was impractical, I decided to bring you into my world. I decided to show you how I communicate with an economist who died nearly 300 years ago.

Suspend your beliefs for a moment and we will talk to Richard Cantillon, considered by many and especially the Austrian Economics School as the founder of modern economics. Come along on an imaginary walk I took with him around downtown Seattle in 2013.

This imaginary technique is how I delve into economics and understand the thoughts of historical economists. It clarifies my understanding of their ideas and embeds them in my memory. This is a basic memory technique. The idea is to move around an environment you know and associate the ideas you want to remember with the places and people you meet along the way.

This book is a recreation of such an imaginary walk I took with Richard Cantillon. To make this technique as relevant as possible I created an imaginary conversation reflecting his knowledge and point of view. He can express his theory in a modern context and I can offer my own perspective. I hope this approach rewards you with a new appreciation of Richard Cantillon's contribution to economics, and a sense of how we can build upon his ideas to create a better economic system.

I use a fictional economist, Peter Barrie, to play my role. Enjoy.

Rand McGreal, September 1, 2013

The Meeting

I glared at my lazy computer screen. The obstinate beast was snoozing with its eyes shut. *How would I ever finish my book on Richard Cantillon? — Even if I finished it, would the book attract readers or repel them? After all he was a banker. And a ridiculously rich banker at that.*

Could I even explain his economic theory? Did I really understand him? Could I get inside his mind? Could I explain to the world, how he might unlock their personal door to wealth and abundance? Surely, people would listen to the man called the first modern economist—an economist acknowledged by Adam Smith as the originator of economic study. He certainly has earned a place on the soap box. He revealed the mystery of economic bubbles. He used his knowledge to become one of the richest people in Europe. Would the fact that he lived 300 years ago discourage digitized brains from appreciating his wisdom?

I could imagine a violent reaction to his ideas—ideas sure to cause agitation in liberal sanctuaries. Those busy hives stretched from Berkeley to the computer bugs in Silicon Valley, and even farther south to the hot bods of Hollywood and Silicone Valley. The liberal drones protecting those porticos of academic arrogance would surely swarm, attack, and devour such an intruding presence. A presence that symbolized the market system.

What was I in for?

Really, Peter, you are in trouble! How can you get computer age people to embrace a horse and buggy economist?

***

Tuesday I had business in Seattle. I arrived in the fog on a late morning ferry, and dragged my weakened mind up to the Merchant's Café for an early lunch. The drizzly spring morning further soaked my suppressed optimism. I had a couple of hours to waste before my appointment. The idea of spending some time in thoughtless oblivion lightened my mental load — my mood always improved with procrastination, and eating was my preferred method to waste an hour. I hated eating alone, so I often sought out a cozy restaurant for company.

I went to the Merchant's Café since the place is convenient to the ferry terminal and close to the IRS offices I had to visit later. As I walked I pushed my hands deeply into my coat pockets and wrapped my coat tighter against the slick pick-pocketing chill. It was late morning and it was still cold. A solitary wisp of fog hung stationary in the alley next to the Café as I approached. I entered and selected a table just inside the door. At the time I didn't realize it, but this was a choice that would change my life.

I slumped into my chair with a sigh. The journey to reach this food palace was long enough. No sense delaying my reward. I looked for a waitress, but I did not see or hear anyone. The Merchant's Café is a late night place for serious drinking. I surmised that the staff was in the back, sitting around a vinyl top table, wrapping their hands around warm coffees, shaking out their personal cobwebs—only rising reluctantly, after expiration of the normal constitutional delay enforced on early arriving customers. Only when the commotion of a customer entering had died to silence would a staff person amble out.

The glory days of the Café had passed in the 1950s. The gory days of the Café had expired in the 1850s. Today the restaurant and bar clung to the notoriety of its ghost visitors and its dubious distinction as the oldest bar in a city built by drunken loggers.

The heavy entry door behind me grudgingly groaned open. A wet victim of Seattle's climate walked in a couple of steps and slowly unbuttoned his overcoat. He stood right in front of me. Thank god, he didn't shake himself off like a dog. He looked around, apparently surprised that the restaurant was so empty. He deepened his scan, searching for a hostess. No luck. He slowly removed a knit cap and let his long gray-blond hair fall onto his shoulders. He stood up straight and commanding as he peered into the corners of the building. His entrance was quite different from my slouching–damn–another–rainy–day arrival.

"The staff is in back," I volunteered, trying to be helpful without intruding.

"Have you been helped?" the stranger asked.

"Not yet," I acknowledged in a flat monotone. I observed his attire more closely and considered rethinking my welcoming remark.

The stranger turned and leaned toward me. "I am new to this country. I am unfamiliar with the customs," he offered in a British accent.

"Are you from merry old England?" I asked.

"My name is Richard, which is English, but I am half Irish and half French, Norman really. Ah, do you mind if I ask you a question about your American customs?"

"Sure, what is it?" I replied, disappointed I didn't get a response to my clever remark.

Richard's face seemed drawn in as he began. "I have had some bad luck and I am just looking for a dry place out of the rain. Will the pub owners allow me to sit here for a moment?"

"I doubt it. They expect you to pay for your seat—by buying something."

"*Sacre bleu!* Then I better clench my teeth and head back out." He started to button his overcoat in preparation for departure.

Considering that he brought improvement to the dingy oak-coffin aesthetic of the Café, I said, "Why don't you share my table with me? They won't throw you out since I'm going to purchase lunch, if anyone ever shows up to take my order."

"That is very generous, but I must tell you I am a fugitive."

That was a surprising comment. Who was this guy? "You don't look like a fugitive. You must be kidding me."

"I am not kidding you. I am a fugitive from the Charlies."

"The Charlies, who are they?" I inquired in a confused tone.

"Ah, they are the London police force created by Charles II."

Believing the likelihood of a London policeman walking through the door remote, I inquired half facetiously, "What are you a fugitive from?"

"The justice system."

I could not quite believe what I was hearing, and it was more than the smooth English accent. Here was a large and imposing man with grey hair who looked respectable enough and spoke like an educated person.

Intrigued I responded, "We're all avoiding the justice system. What's your offense?"

"I am the target of false charges, because I am wealthy."

"That's a crime here, too."

My concerns reduced for the moment, I offered, "Please sit down and dry out. It is extremely unlikely any British police will find you here."

He accepted and pulled out the chair opposite me. I discreetly sniffed the air. All I smelled was the stale odor of beer coming up from the 'historic' oak flooring. I decided to wait before asking him about being a fugitive. "How did you get to the United States?"

"I am afraid I cannot answer that. The last thing I remember is being in Suriname, and then I woke up in the alley just outside this pub. I think there is a portal here."

Totally missing his comment about the portal, I asked, "Were you wearing that overcoat and knit cap on the beach?"

"Ah, no, I got those at a shelter for lost souls last night."

Oh great, a street person.

"That was nice of them to equip you for Seattle, although they should've taken you to REI for some Gore-Tex."

"What is Gore-Tex?"

"Sir, you have a serious gap in your knowledge. You need to know about Gore-Tex, if you're going to hang around here. It's a type of fabric designed for Seattle. It keeps out the rain, but let's your clothing breathe. Let me introduce myself. I'm Peter Barrie. I live on Bainbridge Island. It's an island about five miles west, across the Sound. I took a ferry to come over here this morning. Oh, here comes the waitress."

She greeted us with a hearty, "How're you guys doin' this morning?"

I answered for both of us. "We're glad to be out of the rain and getting something to warm our cockles." The odd English expression seemed to soothe my companion, and was accepted by our waitress without comment. *Apparently, I spoke their language.*

"Can I set you two pups up with a couple of drinks?"

I shook my head no. The waitress reluctantly handed us menus and departed without wasting any more civil words.

"Let's see what we've got here," I said, trying to start a new train of conversation.

My companion reached across the table and offered me his hand. "Nice to meet you, I am Richard – Richard Cantillon."

I was stunned by his name. What a coincidence! Richard Cantillon was the subject of the book I was struggling to write.

When I grabbed his hand to welcome him, I was struck by the coldness of his flesh, but chalked it up to the cold day. I asked, "How do you spell that last name?"

"C..a..n..t..i..l..l..o..n."

The spelling was the same. "Cantillon, that doesn't sound very Irish. In fact, I thought you were French when you used '*sacre bleu*'."

Gathering some comfort from my questions about his name, he settled into the chair. "My family was originally French and I lived most of my life in Paris. My ancestors got to Ireland via the Norman Conquest, but after 500 years and lots of inbreeding the family felt obliged to adopt Ireland as their home."

I answered, "I'm a secondhand Irishman. My father's family originated in Scotland, but traveled to Ireland about the same time as yours." From what I knew of the Cantillon family history, that sounded right. I inquired further: "Do you carry on the family tradition of banking and finance?"

"I was a banker for most of my life."

"Intriguing, I was a banker for a portion of my life. I'm really a finance guy. Usually I ended up managing the capital assets of my employers. I did the analysis of when equipment and real estate needed to be replaced. I now live on the other side of Puget Sound with my wife and daughter. It's a nice life"

"I would enjoy that career."

I was captivated and baffled, but for the moment kept my thoughts to myself. I suggested we look at the menus and we engaged in small talk about what was good in the restaurant until the waitress returned. "What can I get you boys?" she inquired.

Before I could respond, Richard asked where the restroom was located, excused himself and walked away in the direction indicated.

Compensating for the rudeness of my companion, I fabricated an excuse. "He's just feeling a bit queasy," I explained then ordered for both of us. "Let's get two seafood bisques, a loaf of fresh bread, and water to drink." I could tell I was going to get stuck for his meal, but I wanted to hear the fugitive story and more about this Cantillon.

Another part of me began to question what I was doing. *Christ, Peter, you are in Pioneer Square surrounded by the homeless and dangerous! Is this really a good idea? Who is this guy? His accent sounds genuine, but I'm no expert. Could he be a descendent of the Cantillon family just taking on the persona of his famous relative? If so, I might learn something unknown in the historical record. Anyway, he's a more interesting guest than the empty chair at my table that hasn't said a word since I sat down.*

I decided to relax and give it a go for a while longer.

By the time Richard returned our bread was already in a basket on the table. He hunched his shoulders slightly as he leaned across the table and whispered the words I expected.

"I do not have any money. Will they charge me for this bread?"

Feeling generous and willing to pay a few bucks to have my curiosity satisfied, I glibly answered, "Let me get this today, and you can pay me back when you get your feet on the ground."

"Thank you, I will repay you."

I didn't realize at the time how meaningful that statement was. As we waited for our bisque to arrive, I asked, "Are you related to the famous Irish economist, Richard Cantillon?"

"About as close as you can get."

"Really? I'm a great admirer of his economic theories. In fact, I write about modern economic theory and I have a new theory that's similar to something I think he also believed. But a lot has happened since he came up with his idea, so I'm considering a book to update some of his thinking," I said without considering the consequences.

My companion started to smile, but quickly suppressed it. "What are you going to update?"

Realizing I needed to clarify my intent I said, "Now that I think about it, 'update' was a poor word choice. I'm really just trying to get some of his more important ideas recognized as a kind of foundation for what we're learning today. Like the importance of entrepreneurs in growing an economy. Richard Cantillon stressed that economic growth begins with entrepreneurs. He deserves credit for the idea of entrepreneurs as the primary catalyst for economic growth."

"I am not current on recent events, but government has a long history of taking credit for the inventions of entrepreneurs," Richard replied.

My curiosity about this person across from me was growing. *Who am I sitting beside? Is he a mental case pretending to be Richard Cantillon? This part of Seattle is rife with the mentally ill, the homeless, and the lost. Or is there a simpler explanation? Maybe I'm going nuts and just imagining this meeting. Or maybe I'm talking to one of the many apparitions known to haunt this old place. I half-laughed, knowing the owner of the Café would love another ghost story to enhance her marketing. Whoever he was, it was interesting to be talking about an obscure economist that I deeply admired, even if he were actually an escapee from the funny farm. I need to remember this meeting. I do not want to upset my companion by taking notes. Maybe the restaurant name, Merchant Café, will be adequate to trigger my memory of this strange meeting.*

Financial Crisis ABCs

After considering my options, I decided to challenge my lunch companion to see what he knew or could offer about our current economic problems. "Richard, we are trying to escape from a horrible recession. A fifth of our people are unemployed or have taken jobs below their skill level just to feed their families. The economic community is split over the solution. Both sides are adamant in their assertion of their positions. One group follows the theories of John Maynard Keynes, an early twentieth century economist from England, who asserted that more government spending is necessary to kick-start the economy, and the other group is composed of Austrian Economists who argued about the same time that a market economy will steady itself without government intervention."

Richard stared at me for a moment longer than was comfortable and then asked, "How well do you know John Law? He originated the ideas you ascribed to John Maynard Keynes."

"I know he's the Scotsman who promoted the Mississippi Company in the early 18th century, which led to the mother-of-all financial crises and the near bankruptcy of France."

Richard seemed to peer right through me, as though he was looking for my soul. "That is right. He was also the head of the central bank of France, the Royal Bank. In addition, he was appointed Controller-General of Finances, giving him power equivalent to a Prime Minister. Like your John Maynard Keynes, he thought the solution to economic stagnation was to inject the economy with more money."

Recalling my economic history, I said, "I knew he held an office giving him the power to control the currency."

"He had more than power; he was a philosopher-king. He convinced the Regent that his quantity theory of money would rescue France from economic stagnation by keeping interest rates low."

"Low interest rates will do all that?" I joked, trying to lighten the mood.

My effort was in vain. Richard stiffened and drilled his stare through my occipital cavity, across my apparently empty frontal cortex, and into my obviously resting cerebellum, lest I mistake his intention—this was a topic he cared about deeply.

"Peter, John Law used his power at the Royal Bank over the money supply to force interest rates lower. He asserted that the amount of money in the economy determined interest rates. Therefore, he created new paper currency to put more money into the Royal Bank, which according to his theory would stimulate the economy when interest rates dropped. His idea was that the greater the supply of money competing for borrowers, the lower interest rates would be."

"Interesting. That is precisely what our central bank, the Federal Reserve Bank, is doing now to try to stimulate our economy."

Richard asked the pertinent question: "Is it working?"

"Hmm, not very well, and that is surprising since it is the same solution our most respected economist, John Maynard Keynes, gave to extract us from our biggest financial crisis, the Great Depression."

Richard somewhat smugly asked, "How well did it work then?"

"We don't really know, because the process of recovery was interrupted after twelve years when the country entered World War II, and that changed everything."

"Twelve years is a long, long time in an economy. You should know more time would not have changed a thing. Tell Mr. Keynes for me that he is wrong."

"All right, but how do I *explain* to him that he's wrong?"

"You start by telling him there is a difference between money in bank vaults and money in people's pockets."

I thought to myself, one thing is obvious. This apparition, ghost, or time-space traveler knows his stuff. Here I have studied all of Cantillon' writings and read numerous books about him and I've not gotten to this depth of knowledge. Holy cow, if I'm going to write a book about Cantillon I better get to this same level. Pay attention, Peter! You're talking to the subject of your next book.

Richard continued. "The difference is it does not matter how much physical money exists inside state vaults. What matters is how much money is circulating and working in an economy. Think of water as a metaphor for money. If you were lost in the desert with a full canteen of water, what would happen if you could not unscrew the top?"

"Okay, that's clear!"

"Here is another way to think about it. Imagine a simple economy composed of five granaries along a river. All of the granaries depend on the water flow to push their grinding wheels. Now imagine the state has constructed a massive dam to store water at the river's headwaters. Unless, the state releases the water continuously and at the proper rate to push the water wheels, the granaries cannot operate. Water behind the dam is like money in a bank vault. Unless the money is released into an economy it is almost meaningless. A large supply does provide some security and that has value, but it pales in comparison to the force of circulating money. Do people still use the cart before the horse analogy? That is the kind of mistake John Law made and Mr. Keynes is perpetuating."

Richard's clear explanations were compelling, but I felt I should try to defend John Maynard Keynes. I began with my own metaphor. "Keynes believed that an economy in recession is like a cart stuck in the mud. It just needs a push or a pull up onto drier ground and then the cart will move freely. Therefore, the cost to rent a team of horses to pull the cart free is a necessary expense that can be repaid once the cart owner is back in business and making his deliveries."

"Instead of spending money to pull his horses out of difficulty, the merchant should have purchased larger diameter wheels before the rain so he could navigate muddy spots!"

"Okay, I give. You're saying the amount of money created does not matter. It's about spending money on new business ideas and improvements, investments. Did I get that right?"

Richard thoughtfully gazed up at the tin ceiling. He continued, "My belief is that an economic system works best when it is not disturbed. An economy is strengthened when people have the confidence to spend money, and businesses the confidence to invest. So the first thing to do is to restore people's confidence that their money and jobs are secure.

"A government diminishes confidence when it borrows to spend in excess of tax revenues. Deficit spending often endangers the savings of people since inflation usually follows when governments spend beyond their means. People are very aware that all government spending must be repaid with their taxes. Government borrowing means more taxation in future years. This fact diminishes people's enthusiasm for government spending and negates any positive effect of increasing the amount of circulating currency."

"So, is Keynes' approach of adjusting interest rates and government spending ineffective?"

"Yes, it does not work. You have the proof in your last two financial reversals. It is not interest rates, but the willingness of bankers to open up their shells, like the mussels in our soup. Bankers must embrace risk. That willingness nourishes the body of progress. Believing that low interest rates alone are sufficient to convince wise business people to invest is ridiculously naïve."

The waitress returned with our seafood bisque just in time. *I need a break. This is intense, but great! I love the dam metaphor. It illustrates Cantillon's second major idea, that it is business investment and not government monetary manipulations that propels an economy. This is a core principle that I thought I discovered, but at least I have my correlation studies of business investment during the Great Depression to support Cantillon's theory.*

The food was served on white earthenware with carefully hand-drawn lines of deep blue on the rims reminiscent of our locale next to the Pacific Ocean. Richard picked up the large serving spoon from the tray and gulped at the bisque from the tureen. I leaned forward and explained that our personal silverware was wrapped inside our cloth napkins. He flushed red and started to apologize. I waved at him to move past the mistake and suggested we just enjoy the bisque. While we unwrapped our utensils, the waitress returned with a new serving spoon and our personal bowls. We each filled our bowl from the steaming cauldron of spicy seafood and dipped in for a slow savoring spoonful.

"Ooh!" Richard exclaimed. "That is hot!"

"Let's give it a moment," I said.

While we waited for the bubbling, spicy bisque to simmer down, I asked Richard, "When you wrote that 'The celibacy of churchmen is not as disadvantageous as is popularly believed...but their idleness is very harmful,' were you arguing that each person should be employed? I believe the readers of my book about you, and *especially* the unemployed readers, would like to know your opinion."

Richard slowly diverted his stare from his simmering seafood. "Yes, everyone has an obligation to work – even the clergy."

"An obligation or a right?"

"A right and an obligation. When people are not working they are a burden on the rest of society. Regardless of the color or material of the robes you wrap around yourself, or the sacrifices you made to obtain your position, you are still a human. And each human should contribute to the sustenance of the community. I do not demean religious work, but poverty and piety are not a justification to escape the burdens of being a citizen of a community. Everyone must work and the community has an obligation to encourage work opportunities."

I nodded my head in understanding and pointed out to Richard that this was one of the concepts of his *Essai* that I wanted the public to appreciate. "The way I explain this is to clarify that an activity is not productive work unless it provides a service or product to someone else. So an indigent monk is not working by depriving himself, but is working when he brings comfort to the poor and sick. He provides a service when he gives sympathy, but provides no service or product through his ascetic lifestyle. Would you agree with that statement?"

"*Oui*, well said."

We concentrated on slurping for a few minutes. Richard had a very casual posture. He slumped around his plate as he ate like he was protecting his food from unseen guests at the table.

I need to remember this encounter. Let's see. I will use the Richard borrowing money from me as my memory device. He borrows lunch money from me and then tells me money only stimulates the economy if it leaves the bank vault or my wallet.

He says John Law and Keynes are wrong about their belief that a greater amount of money and low interest rates will stimulate the economy, because that can be counteracted by cautious bankers not approving loans.

Finally, Richard spoke about employment as a right and an obligation. The next time we eat together I hope he follows this approach in his use of napkins.

Role of Entrepreneurs

I pondered where to take the conversation and finally asked about something that I had never heard explained. "How did government handle unemployment in the 18th century?"

"What is unemployment?"

"Really, you do not know what unemployment is?"

"No."

"Our waitress in this restaurant will be unemployed if the restaurant burns down or closes for lack of business."

"That sounds like a rare situation. Do you really need a special word for that circumstance?"

"It is not just fires and business circumstances, but for numerous reasons such as competition or the birth of a child that a person can become unemployed. It is a major concern today because we rely on the government to provide sustenance to the unemployed until they can find another source of income. I was just asking if government had a similar role in your time."

"Government was the King. He only engaged soldiers and the household staff for his palaces. Most of these servants were provided by noblemen interested in protecting their lands from plunder by foreigners. Helping the King was a way to protect their property."

Baffled by his answer I probed further, "What happened to the household staff or the soldiers when the King did not need them any longer?"

"They gathered their belongings and returned to the estate from whence they came."

"So there was no unemployment?"

"Not in the way you use the word."

Not ready to give up I continued, "Certainly, there must have been people without a place to sleep or a nice cozy estate to sit down in for dinner?"

"*Oui.*"

"Did the King provide any help to these people?"

"No, nor did they seek it. People not attached to any estate went into the forest or along the rivers to fend for themselves."

"What about in the cities?"

"It was a similar situation."

"People couldn't hunt or fish in the city. How did they survive?

"In the cities there were more opportunities to trade labor or sex for food and lodging, but many people survived on begging or petty robbery."

"That doesn't sound too pleasant."

"Well, it was not as clean and ordered as your city, but it was an exciting time to live. Life was hard, but we had no vision of what we lacked. People did not have money. Coinage was so rare that most people had never even held money. When conditions were bad people did not suffer unemployment, they died!" Richard raised his spoon for emphasis and sent bisque flying in my direction.

I recoiled from the barrage and to gain some distance from the reality of 18th century life. "Was the problem that most people worked in slave-like conditions?" I suggested.

"*Oui.* The economic system had few wealth mechanisms to provide revenue for owners, and even fewer landlords had sufficient income to provide pay for their workers. Everyone lived a communal existence and shared the meager returns of their labor based on their status.

"Ah, but in the cities it was a different situation. There were many jobs, but payment was unreliable. There was a strong connection between the worker and the employer. The employer depended on the worker for his own sustenance. This link meant employers interested in sustaining their businesses worked hard to provide some payment to their employees even when conditions were bad.

"Unfortunately, conditions were more often bad than good, and most workers suffered from inadequate nutrition, clothing, and housing. Some people were naked and lived on alms and the generosity of the church. The problem was not unemployment. It was whether a worker would be paid for his labor at a level sufficient to support his family."

Kroossshh! The front door swung open and crashed against the wall next to us. In walked the dishwasher with a selection of face hardware that rivaled Home Depot's small metal parts aisle. Below his bald crown every spot of loose skin was pierced with a ring, stud, or bauble. He had a ring in his thick lower lip, another couple of rings buried in his dense bushy eyebrows, three rings of different sizes hanging from the septum of his nose, large rings hanging from his nipples visible under the bright yellow tee shirt stretched tightly over his bulky tattooed chest. A large stud in the shape of an avocado flicked back and forth on his tongue as he entered panting like a dog. A small spoon dangled from his left ear and a small fork from his right ear. Large knife tattoos stretched the length of each forearm.

Richard stared at the man as he headed toward the back of the restaurant. "Is he a pirate?"

"In a way. Richard, I know from the appearance of this restaurant it looks like we have not advanced much, but believe me, most ships today are not manned by pirates. He's not showing off his occupation, but his defiance of what you and I stand for."

"Ah, he got my attention. Message understood, fellow," Richard muttered.

I returned to the difficulty of paying workers a sufficient wage. "How could business even survive under the conditions you described?"

Richard set down his spoon and wiped his face with his napkin. "It was difficult, and most business ventures failed, but there was no other option. That is why I wrote in my *Essai* that 'income must be sufficient to support a worker.' An economic system that cannot provide incomes sufficient for people to prosper and support themselves fails its social obligation. The powerlessness of workers in my time was a real concern. Certainly, people could stop working, but they lacked savings and other resources to assert their right to a wage sufficient for living. The monarchy in France ignored this problem, but took advantage of all the cheap labor," Richard lamented as painful memories deepened the creases descending from his cheek-bones to his lower jaw. "The monarchy ignored the obvious assertion of the poor classes that 'everyone must live' and that to do so required a sufficient wage." Richard frowned. "If the French monarchy is ever overturned it will be for this reason."

Playing off Richard's comment I asked, "Do you think government should be responsible for finding jobs for people?"

"Ah, *oui*, in a manner. Government should ensure the conditions for others to create jobs. Not everyone is a job creator. Government does not create permanent jobs, only entrepreneurs do. Government should improve the conditions for entrepreneurs to be successful. This is the best action government can take to increase the number of jobs"

"You're stating your idea that entrepreneurs are the creative force in an economy and the only group with the capability to see new business opportunities. You look at government as lacking that skill, so how should government and entrepreneurs coordinate?"

"I would start in the schools and emphasize making things and deemphasize memorizing things.

Knowing the names and length of reigns of all the Kings from Philip II to Louis XIV is an impressive demonstration of intellectual capacity, but it will not feed or clothe anyone. Our schools need to teach all the advancements of mankind up to the current moment. This will teach students how to think by learning the patterns and techniques employed by the great thinkers of the past. This is the technique used in the Guilds. It works wonderfully and should be followed in all schools."

Since Richard's answer brought up a problem facing many countries today, I asked, "After you have an educated population, how do people get jobs?"

"Good question, my friend. Most people think education creates jobs, but jobs are created by entrepreneurs. I hate to be repetitive, but that is an important concept. This is the difference between a wealthy country and a poor country. Spain is a poor country and England is a rich country because Spain has no culture of entrepreneurship and England does.

"It should be the other way around. Spain has broad plains of grassland for raising stock. Spain has a good source of water draining off the Pyrenees. England has wet, swampy, slimy meadows that produce one miserable crop of grass per year. Spain has sunshine all year to grow fruits and vegetables. England has overcast skies every month of the year. Spain has vast gold and silver wealth from the New World. England possesses a colony that only produces foul smelling cigars. Yet England is the rich country. Unusual, is it not?"

"I've always sought a simple explanation for why, after Spain looted all the gold and silver of the New World, the country and especially its government remained impoverished and short of currency.

"At the time, in the 18th century, political people thought that hoards of gold and silver in a country's treasury would ensure a booming economy, but that didn't occur. Richard, is there a simple explanation?"

"*Oui*, the answer is simple, but composed of a couple of parts. Spain spent its gold buying foreign imports and gilding churches—not building businesses inside the country. For comparison, look at England—they did the opposite. England supported the entrepreneur. In my time, Parliament ran the government, not the Monarchy. Parliament encouraged business. It is the English entrepreneur that made England rich. Spain had few entrepreneurs.

"The *Hildago* culture in Spain discouraged wealthy nobles from business development. The *Hildago* culture stressed a life of leisure. Nobles avoided business activity just as they shunned manual labor. They believed their noble birth would be dishonored if they engaged in the activities of the businessman."

"Let me think about that," I said, realizing that Richard's long explanations had prevented him from eating his bisque.

What ideas of Cantillon did we discuss? First, the idea that unemployment can only be solved through new business creation. Second, that only entrepreneurs have the capability to originate new business concepts. Third, that the level of entrepreneurship in a country determines its economic vitality. That is an impressive list! How can I tie those thoughts to a tattooed, pierced cook who interrupted our discussion when he crashed through the door?

Maybe it is not so hard. Only a clever entrepreneur could make a business out of body piercings and then find jobs for people so adorned. Hooray for entrepreneurship!

Investing

Noticing that Richard had nearly finished his bisque, I started in again. "You have very interesting insights about entrepreneurs and their role in business creation. Would you mind if I ask you some questions about your own wealth?"

"Go right ahead," Richard said, dipping into his bisque in pursuit of the last golden mussels swimming away from their cramped black cells. Richard was not very graceful, but extremely determined in his chase of the savory bivalve. His zeal had left a substantial stain on the tablecloth. *Richard must be a relative of Cantillon, at least. I've never heard of a ghost with a ravenous appetite like this apparition possesses.*

"Is it true that you were the richest person in Europe at the start of the 18th century?"

Richard, eye-to-eye with the mussel in his spoon, said "That is a charge many people brought to avoid paying their debts to me," then quickly swallowed his last briny victim.

"Are you ashamed of your wealth?"

"Not at all. Wealth is derived from hard work. I earned every shilling."

"Do you believe there is a connection between work and money?"

"Absolutely. Monetary expansion should follow product expansion and if it does not keep up, the economy staggers. Every farmer and craftsman should be able to exchange his work for money. In the 18th century that was a problem. There was never enough coinage to meet the need. Fortunately for me, the governments of Europe, by failing to meet the currency needs of their economies, left a gap for banks to capitalize. The failure of governments to look beyond their own needs created the opportunity for banks. Bankers solved the problem of too little coinage by creating accounts and booking deposits."

Suddenly, everything went dark. "Hey, Peter, what are you doin' in the big citeee? The huge muscular black man standing behind me slowly took his heavily callused hands off my eyes, but only after shaking my head side to side a couple of times and teasing my hair so it stood up in an unruly mess.

"Hey, hey, hey," I shouted as he shoved his elbows into my shoulders and played with my hair.

"Richard, this is my...very bad friend, Azure Brown." Azure took his hands off me and reached over my head and across the table to grab and shake Richard's hands.

Richard rose still holding Azure's hand. "Glad to make your acquaintance."

Azure grabbed Richard's hand like a bear serves himself at the buffet table. The force of Azure's two-handed grip and vigorous shaking lifted the substantial Irishman nearly on to his feet.

"Glad to meet yuh, buddy!"

"Azure, take a seat and join us. This is Richard Cantillon, the famous Irish economist."

"An economist, just like my little buddy here," Azure noted, giving me an extremely hardy back slap not once, but twice.

Have yuh read his book, tha *Rule of Money*?"

"Not yet."

"It has this theory about money as earnings. And if people work they should be entitled to earnings or money. So muthers who work at home get paid by a company that monitors what they teach. Cool, huh? It helps poor countries a lot, too."

"It sounds revolutionary."

"Oh, yeah!"

"Thanks for promoting my book. Richard, I met Azure not long after I graduated from college, while I was on a mountain climbing trip to Yosemite Valley. We both needed money and heard about this mining job in the 'mountains' north of LA. Since fall was turning into winter we headed down there. The job was at a lapis lazuli mine near San Bernardino. The seam went vertically from the canyon bottom to the ridge top. We dug out the lapis with picks and then we had to haul out bags of the blue ore in backpacks, because the mine was in a Wilderness Area. This is how Henry here became Azure. I wanted to name him Cucamonga after the Wilderness Area, but he liked Azure better."

"The truth is, Peter wanted to name me Cucamonga because he thought I was cuckoo."

"We worked there all winter. It was one of the best times of my life. And I shared it with this crazy guy."

Azure chimed in, "I liked tha weather. Then I followed Peter up to this slimy wet jungle to climb, and than he introduced me to my gurl and here I am. Oh, there's my friend. I need to go. Nice meeting you guys, bye." In a flash Azure was a memory.

Azure met his friend and went straight to the bar to have drinks.

"What were we talking about?" I asked.

Richard said, "I had just mentioned that banks exploited the opportunity created when governments failed to issue sufficient currency to enable commerce.

This failure led in part to both the Mississippi and South Sea Bubbles. Government's superficial understanding of business causes many unnecessary economic disruptions. Since governments create markets by their dominating presence, or by their regulations, as an individual businessperson you have no choice except to participate.

"Many people who made investments with me in the Mississippi Company did not understand the simplest business concept and lost a great deal of money as a result. They did not appreciate that people can rapidly change their opinion of the value of a share, not only when the share price is going up, but also when it is going down."

"How were prices determined?

"In those days it was a negotiation between buyers and sellers, which is the proper way to arrive at price agreement. At times I acted as a broker for the government and sold shares on commission."

"Is that why you are a fugitive?"

"In a way it is, yes, but that is not the whole story."

"Tell me about the Mississippi Company and what other mistakes investors made."

"Ah, to be an investor in shares of the Mississippi Company required you to know the difference between an option and an investment. The shares John Law sold were primarily options because at the time there were no profits to support a value for the Company. In fact, the shares were being sold based on rumors perpetuated by the Company and its marketing agents. One incident I recall: the newspaper, *Nouveau Mercure,* ran an article stating the new city of New Orleans consisted of 800 fine houses and five parishes, but my brother after he visited reported to me the city contained a hundred random huts, one store built of wood, and two or three houses of extremely low quality."

"Did the government plant that lie?"

"Yes. In such a situation you buy shares on the possibility of benefiting from a possible rise in share prices. It is pure speculation. You have the 'opportunity' to buy at a low price before the real value is determined. Opportunity is the key concept. Many investors treated their purchase of shares in the Mississippi Company like ownership of a piece of a company rather than like a lottery ticket that might or might not pay off."

Richard paused and surveyed his surroundings. "See those globes hanging from the ceiling?" he said, pointing to a pair of large stained glass light fixtures that hung at the back the restaurant. "Those are not right for an English pub."

Brilliant observation, Richard! You died one hundred years before electricity was discovered. I knew that Darby, the bar owner, would greatly resent his criticism of her carefully collected antiques, most of which she discovered lost in the dusty musty aisles of Goodwill.

Richard returned to the topic, apparently not expecting me to comment on his decorating viewpoint. "Remember, the Mississippi Company was just a holding company granted monopoly rights by the French government to develop the Mississippi delta. "When many investors looked at their Company stock certificates I am sure they pictured the pile of gold they had exchanged for the jungles of the Mississippi waiting to be invested. The problem with that vision was that the gold went to the creators of the opportunity. The investors had merely purchased an opportunity.

"At the time, I went along with the crowd and purchased that same opportunity. The difference is that I became rich, and they lost all their money. Why, *savoir faire*? I succeeded because I saw my shares as a speculative opportunity. When prices moved up I waited for my opportunity to sell. As prices increased 1000% I saw my 'opportunity' – I sold and made a profit. I acted as a speculator, not an investor. I realized the shares only had lasting value if commercial trade developed. When I saw that trade was not developing as expected, I sold."

"How were you able to sell at the right time?"

"I did not sell at the perfect time. The market went up a great deal more after I sold. I sold when a change in direction was first visible. But the people who invested alongside me maintained a belief in a commercial bonanza long after all the evidence was contrary. They even ignored my advice to sell. They did not see their investment as an opportunity, but as a pile of shares worth more money each day during the boom. I would ask them why their shares were worth more and they would answer, because people will pay more for them. When you let other speculators determine the value of an investment you are *fait accompli.*

"True investments are products priced according to their returns. Investments that return more with the same risk profile are worth more. This is why stock prices go up. Companies over time typically show a greater and greater ability to earn profits. This was the case with the Mississippi Company for a while, but as time passed and the actual difficulty of profiting from their trade monopoly became apparent, the value of the shares should have fallen.

"That, unfortunately, is not how many investors understood their holdings. They saw them as increasing in value every day, because that is what yesterday's trading price indicated. An investor must ignore the market and evaluate the prospects of a company in the real world. Even a monopoly will fail if it has no product to sell. At the end of the day the Mississippi Company had monopoly rights to restrict competition, but no products to sell. The Mississippi

Company was not a fraud, but a failure of naïve investors to properly evaluate the potential."

"Why didn't a viable commerce develop and the Mississippi Company survive as a trading company?"

"North America at the time was not occupied by people who made products like in the Far East. They only produced enough to support their tribal community. They had a need for our products, but there was nothing of value to purchase from them in trade."

Interested in the real world of the 18th century, I wanted to know how people reacted to losing fortunes. "When people lose the kind of sums lost in the Mississippi Company, some often try to extract revenge. Did some of those investors you financed to purchase shares come after you?"

Richard smiled. "Ah, still looking for an answer to your fugitive question. I will not parry you anymore. Yes, they did."

"Did they try to kill you?"

"Some had that intention, but most just wanted to sue me to prevent my collection of what they owed me. With the corruption of the judiciary, it was less expensive to pay off a judge than pay off their debts to me."

"Is that why you say you are a fugitive?"

Richard gave me an arm wave that might have meant "No" but looked more like the arm movement of a traffic cop. I wondered exactly what that evasive wave could mean, but decided to ignore it for now.

Just then, a huge crash of glassware reverberated through the restaurant. A very distraught young waitress stared down at the floor. The sparkling shards of glass seemed so out of place on the dark stained wood floor near the bar. The crash brought out the curious from the backroom.

I noticed the restaurant employee population had suddenly grown – apparently more staff had arrived unnoticed by me for the afternoon shift and dinner preparation. Some of the tables were dressed with tablecloths and had place settings. Another waitress was storing cases of beer and wine in cubbies behind the counter. A hostess was stationed at her desk by the front door. She was looking at her computer and using a wax crayon to make notes on the seating chart. Gradually the stunned crowd standing outside the kitchen door began to bend over and help the young waitress remove the mess.

I turned to Richard. "Are restaurants in England this exciting?"

"Not as dangerous. We do not have glass drinking containers. Ours are pottery tankards or pewter cups. I noticed something similar on the shelf above the bar. See those pottery figures?" Richard pointed to a row of Toby Jugs.

"Do you know what those are?" I asked.

"No, but those colorfully glazed ceramics are similar to the mugs and tankards we use in pubs."

I pushed my chair back. "Stand up. I want you to get a better of view of the jugs. Let's walk over to the bar and I'll ask the waitress to take a couple off the shelf." Richard reluctantly followed me to the bar. The waitress lifted down two of the jugs.

Richard's lips parted into a big smile.

"Do you recognize these people?" I said holding a tankard up for Richard to see. "We call these seated beer drinkers Toby Jugs. I think it is a reference to a drunkard in a Shakespearean play, but I am not sure. He is wearing 18th century attire, isn't he?" I smiled mischievously at Richard.

He picked up one of the jugs and turned it around and around, admiring the silly attire and tri-cornered hat that served as a pouring spout. In jest he asked, "Is this how you amuse yourselves, by poking fun at our dear Royals?"

"I am sure that the tradition began with your relatives and we are just continuing the custom!"

"Very amusing. I can see that drinking culture has not changed. In my time we did not break glassware, but jugs of grog were thrown back and around. It was usually the patrons causing a row. In its appearance this restaurant is not much different from a modern pub in England. It has the delicate molded plaster ceilings and heavy oak booths and walls panels. Although, I have never seen anything like that huge hog-sized serving tray the young woman dropped."

"You didn't have trays?"

"We have small trays. When I was a young man I saw a small silver tray called a 'salver' used to place food on the table for royalty. Food placed on a salver had been tested for poisons and thus was deemed safe for Royals to eat. Your use of trays is much more practical."

"By practical do you mean 18th century practical?"

"*Oui.*"

For Richard's benefit, I clarified a few details about the history of the Merchant Café. "This restaurant was built in the mid-19th century, and the ceiling is not molded plaster, but a poor copy made out of thin metal panels with a pattern pressed into the surface to look like plaster. We call this architectural trick a tin ceiling."

"It fooled me."

The waitress interrupted us to ask, "Do you two young men want some dessert?" Of course, my companion jumped at the question and asked if she had a crumble.

"No, but I have a Halloween Booberry crisp, which is similar." Before I could deflect my companion he'd ordered a dish. Begrudgingly, I decided to join him in spending my money.

After our waitress floated away, I leaned over to Richard and asked him why he had ordered dessert.

"Ooooh," he said. "Not included?"

Realizing his mistake his confidence slumped and he began an animated apology. *"Mon Dieu,* I am so sorry. I did not realize. I am surprised by the additional charge. I can catch her. I can cancel the order. Let me make an apology. Please..."

Richard continued to plead to correct his misstep and not until I had accepted his apology ten times did he stop.

I squeezed my eyes shut and thought about how I could remember this discussion. *I can connect my mining adventure to Richard's idea of monetary expansion matching product expansion. The value of the lapis mine increased with each new seam of ore uncovered. Next, Richard's discussion of the difference between stock speculation and stock investment in the Mississippi Bubble can easily be tied to the crash of the glassware tray.*

Money

"Richard, forget about the booberry crisp—gluttony is acceptable in my book."

"Peter, please leave that out of the book."

"Your secret is safe with me. I am sorry, I over-reacted. Let's just eat the blueberries and then I'll take you on a brief tour of the city while I'm on my way to drop off some papers."

"I would enjoy a tour, but how can I make up for my blunder? I feel so bad."

"Richard, you can repair the damage by dropping the subject, and simply enjoying your berries when they arrive. It's nothing to me; I was just confused by your action. Sorry. Please explain your idea that money is only a medium of exchange."

"All right, but I am making a note that I owe you the price of the berries."

Richard paused to collect his thoughts before answering. "Ah money... The main point about money is that it is not wealth. I think of money as closer to a letter-of-credit than a gold bar. Money is a certificate of value. It is not a valuable object itself, but a stored value that the government legislates must be accepted in exchange for a product.

"Imagine money in the center of an equation bracketed with equal signs. On either side of the equal signs is a product. The first product is the product to be sold to the money holder and the other product is the product he wants to purchase. This is one of the most important ideas from my *Essai*. It is the idea money must originate with a product. Many governments break this rule to their great detriment when they just print more money as needed."

"Or nowadays when the government prints new money to spur the economy by lowering interest rates."

"*Oui*, since money is only a certificate of value representing the first product, it is contrary to economic principles to issue more money without more products to justify it. To do so causes inflation or debases the currency, which is the same thing."

I was excited. "Unbelievable! This is similar to a principle I discovered in 2011! But instead of associating money creation with a product, I associate it with earnings. The catchy phrase I use is 'money must be earned.' I call this principle the Rule of Money. The idea is that money should not be created by a sovereign government. Money creation should originate with work or, as you state in your book, product making.

"I am sure you can see the significance of this idea. All work earns a monetary credit that can be exchanged for products. Instead of the government printing money based on interest rates and doling it out to castle builders and their defenders and friends, money should be distributed in a mechanical way, as the market requires it, in salaries to people making products or providing services. Work becomes the main reward strategy, not who you know or what you look like. Are we thinking alike?" I asked hopefully.

Richard slowly responded, "That is a lot to absorb. It never occurred to me to make the leap to earnings, but I see no logical reason to dispute your contention. In fact, the more I think about your idea, the more I like it. Even though you did not know about my idea that money creation must begin with a product, you reached a similar conclusion.

"When people ask why the first money was created, the obvious answer is that money follows creation of a product. There is no reason for money until someone wants to carry away their earnings from a product sale, rather than carry away another product. Money is the first improvement beyond barter. Money is just a substitute for a product, a placeholder.

"Peter, let me ask you a question about your idea: how does redefining money change an economy? What would this new economic world look like? I can't see how it would change the 18th century."

I said, "Here is where we have a difference. While you say money is a commodity, I say it is a concept. The significance of this difference is that a commodity is subject to the rules of supply and demand. A concept is not subject to the rules of supply and demand. So in my world the quantity of money can expand forever and ever as long as people continue to work and earn."

Richard rubbed the underside of his strong chin while I continued excitedly. The main point of my own economic theory was being reviewed by the originator of the field. "When money is subject to the rules of supply and demand, the amount of money created has consequences such as inflation. When money is a concept, the amount of new money matches new work. Consequently, there is no inflation since there is no excess. The quantity paid matches the quantity earned and needed."

Richard wiped his lips in preparation for dessert. He asked, "Are you saying that as long as a bank or a country follows your rules of monetary expansion there will be no inflation?"

"No inflation caused by printing money. Prices will increase when manufacturers include new features or their cost of production increases."

Richard paused, thinking. I elaborated, "Each new dollar must be created to pay for new work. Money must be earned. On the other hand, any dollar printed by government to pay for a new wing on the palace is inflationary, since it is not earned in a market transaction. Listen closely—a market transaction only occurs between a buyer and seller, and the seller must earn the money he gets from the buyer by providing a product or service. When a King or oligarch spends for his own use it breaks the economic circle. It does not increase productivity or reward productive people. Such expenditures take value out of the economic circle. The King is happier, but the monetary resources of the economy are misused."

Richard's brow creased in pensive consideration of my confident answer. "That is a strong argument. Let's say you are right. How would using your monetary approach change how an economy works?"

"Well, it wouldn't change the banking industry. Banking only expands the money supply when funding a new business. The biggest change would occur in the provision of public services like medical care and education."

The waitress arrived with our blueberry crisp, and Richard swooped in. No sooner had the serving plate crinkled the tablecloth than Richard's index finger was up to the second knuckle in blueberries and returning to his mouth for a taste.

"How is the crisp?" I asked.

"Delicious, exactly like a crumble. I like the raisins and nuts on top."

"How long has it been since you ate...one in an English pub?"

"It must have been more than twenty years. I am extremely fuzzy on time these last couple of days. I feel like I got hit on the head and woke up after a decade in a coma."

I jumped at this opportunity. "What is the last thing you remember?"

"I remember sitting in the library of my house in Suriname, getting drowsy, and nothing after that."

"Do you remember the year?"

"Not exactly, but it was after 1750. I remember my sixtieth birthday."

"Do you realize it is 2013 now?"

"That is very confusing. I can tell that I am in the future by the people and the things around me, but I do not know how or why this should be. I feel like I just woke up in a new world. I remember being in Suriname yesterday."

"Intriguing. Do you have any sense of how people now regard your ideas and contributions to economic thought?"

"I hope they have a good opinion of me."

"They do. You are considered the originator of political economy theory."

"What is that?"

"Political economy theory is the study of how public policy affects the performance of the economy to produce jobs, wealth, products, and services. The idea is that the laws and regulations of the state affect the outcomes of the economic system."

Richard smiled. "I am glad I started that discussion. It is humbling to be considered one of the founders of economics. As I noted in my book, *Essai,* government actions such as taxes impoverish people, regulations impoverish people, war impoverishes people, and debt impoverishes people. These are the four main actions of government that need to be restrained. Has that changed?"

"The lack of change is one of the shocking aspects about meeting you. We are still dealing with the same political problems that you dealt with. We have a government that thinks it needs to oversee every action anyone takes. Were you opposed to big government?"

"Do I breathe air? Of course I am opposed to big government. Big government is primarily interested in its own wellbeing. It will try to trick you into thinking it is interested in your wellbeing, and it is to a point, but only to the extent that you help secure its power. Big government splits the population into groups and doles out favors to certain groups to secure allegiance. As my good friend Voltaire said, 'In general, the art of government consists of taking as much money as possible from one class of citizens to give to another.' I hope that aspect has changed."

I replied regretfully, "Governments still concentrate on what is best for their supporters and not the overall vitality of the country. No one in government is looking at how to improve the efficiency of what it does. The entire focus is on what it can give to its followers to ensure continued support. It is government based on buying votes."

"The Sun King ruled the roost when I worked in Paris. I visited the nest of his eminence at the Palace of Versailles and witnessed the unrestrained hubris of a man who called himself the state: *'l' Etat, c'est moi!'* When you spend the resources of your country on a playground for yourself and your lieutenants, you are clearly not interested in the welfare of your citizenry or country. How modestly does your leader live?"

Our waitress approached and said, "It sounds like you two are having an engrossing conversation. Can I get you anything else?"

I responded to the attractive woman, "The blueberries were delightful. I guess we are ready for our check."

"Sure, do you want to pay with a card?"

"Yes, let me give it to you," I answered, reaching for my back pocket. I pulled out my credit card from my wallet and gave it to the waitress who left to add up our bill.

Richard waited for the waitress to approach the payment terminals at the end of the bar and then leaned over and asked, "How do you pay with a card?"

"Oh yeah, a credit card transaction would be of interest to an 18th century banker. It works this way. Banks make credit cards and send them out to their customers. Each credit card has a unique number embossed on the face of the card that can be read by a machine. The waitress takes the card to the terminal and swipes it across the reader. The reader automatically contacts the bank and tells the bank, 'Peter wants to borrow some money to pay for his lunch.' The terminal at the bank checks my account and says yes or no. If the answer is yes the restaurant terminal turns on and allows the waitress to enter the cost of the lunch and print a receipt.

"In a few moments the waitress will return with a receipt for me to sign. Oh, here she comes now. The receipt will be in the black folder she is carrying."

"Here you go, Mr. Barrie. I hope you have a pleasant afternoon. Thanks for dining with us."

The waitress put the black credit card folder on the table and smiled at each of us. We both thanked her. I picked up the credit card receipt and handed it to Richard for him to peruse. He read both sides thoroughly including the offer for free Happy Hour *hors d'oeuvres* on the back. Richard handed back the receipt and I signed it.

"Do you always have to borrow money to pay for lunch?"

"Not always, but often enough that I am never without a credit card," I admitted. "People usually use a credit card in a restaurant, because they want a record of the expense for their taxes. A business lunch purchased for a client can be a tax-deductible expense.

"It's time for us to leave. Put on your coat and let's go."

I realized I had totally crossed over. My Richard Cantillon was very real. His ideas reverberated through the centuries. But I needed to remember some of the stuff we had discussed.

I can recall this discussion about money because it occurred just before I paid the bill. That is a second memory connection to money in the Merchant Café. The first was Richard's borrowing, the second is my paying our bill. I will associate paying with the introduction of my monetary theory that money creation should occur when a new product or service is offered for sale. It is at that moment that more money is needed to support the economy. This differs from current monetary policy in which money is created to spur the economy.

Richard was hesitant, but ultimately receptive of this idea. I wonder if he will ask me more about my idea?

Monetary Policy

I pushed my chair back. We both stood up. Richard wrapped his emerald green scarf around his neck and pulled on his gray knit hat.

I pulled on my tour guide persona. "Let's walk up the hill to the tallest building in the city, once home to the largest bank in the state. It's over 70 stories tall. The building was called Seafirst Tower when it opened, but now it is called Columbia Center. We're going up to a floor called the Sky View Observatory where we'll have a 360-degree view of the city."

Richard nodded, acknowledging the itinerary, and headed toward the crosswalk where he quickly stepped across the curb onto Yesler Way.

I grabbed the bulky sleeve of his black overcoat and pulled him back up onto the sidewalk. "Richard! Come this way. We need to walk up the hill first. It's only a couple of blocks."

Leading my tour group of one, we headed straight up the hill toward the white terracotta face of Smith Tower. I recalled for him that it was the tallest building west of the Mississippi River until 1962 when the Space Needle exceeded it. We walked through misty rain, which collected in the places where the old sidewalk did not drain. Richard seemed to have no problem climbing the steep hill, but then he unexpectedly sighed as we moved away from the old brick buildings of Pioneer Square

"Is that the building we are going to?" he asked, looking up at the Smith Tower.

"Uh, no, look up this way; see that large black building peeking up over there? We'll be on top of that in a few moments." My companion's pace slowed. I asked, "Does that bother you?"

"Sorry, but the height of these buildings does make me a bit dizzy. It is like being in the Hall of Mirrors at Versailles: I cannot adjust to the depth of the space. I guess I am just unable to sort out what I am looking at. Can we go inside soon?"

"Certainly, a little more than a three blocks and we will be at the front door."

We reached the top of the hill and gazed across Fourth Avenue at the grand staircase leading to Seattle's City Hall. I explained that this was where the Mayor of Seattle worked.

"An imposing stairway to climb to meet the Mayor, a *pastiche* of a Mayan temple. Does the Mayor want the citizenry to supplicate at his feet?"

"Be kind, Richard. Our Mayor is a common man, but his architects may've had a grander vision of the importance of the office."

We crossed the street and walked along the sidewalk in front of City Hall next to a pond of small water spouts. The technology of the fountain did not faze Richard. He took it in as quite normal. Maybe water fountain technology had not advanced much since the 18th century.

We crossed Cherry Street and came upon the maroon granite pedestal walls of Columbia Tower, our destination. Richard looked up at the glass tower rising above us. The view unsteadied him, but when he shifted his perspective to the walls in front of us he regained his balance. In another twenty steps the sidewalk pavers opened up into an entry alcove. The ceiling above us relaxed Richard and recharged his curiosity. "What is this black wall made of?" he asked as he reached across a knee-high planter filled with a low hedge of euonymus and tapped the glass panel.

"That is just a piece of glass painted black on the inside."

"It must be twenty feet long. I have never seen a piece of glass that big. The largest piece of glass I ever saw was in the stained glass windows of the Cathedral Notre Dame in Paris, and I am sure it was no longer than my forearm."

As we walked alongside the painted window Richard reached out again and tapped it harder. "What makes it so solid?"

"The glass is thick. It's probably a solid half inch. If you look up you'll see that much of the outside wall of the building is glass. We'll be looking out those windows in ten minutes. Let's go in here."

We crossed the brick pavers into the alcove at the southwest corner of the building. I pushed open one of the double doors for Richard and he dashed through. I appreciated his change in attitude.

I held the door open and called him back. "Hey, Richard, look at this. This door is made from a solid piece of glass. Feel how thick it is."

My student eagerly gripped the door edge and marveled at its weight and thickness. For a moment it seemed like the tour might end at this fascinating door. But after scanning the entire surface Richard entered the inner lobby and we proceeded toward the escalator. I realized this would require some explanation before he jumped on board.

"Richard, hold up." I grabbed his shoulder and stopped him. "Do you see the people up ahead getting on that moving stair? Let's watch them for a moment. The moving stair is called an escalator. It's a common way of getting people from one level of a building to another, but getting on and off can be a bit tricky. See how people put their foot completely on a step. They do not step on the crack. That's very important. See how the steps separate as they ascend. If you step on a crack you will fall off as the step moves up. The other thing to remember is to balance by holding the handrail."

Richard seemed not to have heard my explanation; he was distracted by something more interesting. "Did you see the shoes that the tall woman was wearing? She is walking around balanced on a tiny heel spike. How does she do that?"

"Some things defy explanation. Are you ready to attempt the escalator? I'll go right behind you to hold you up if you fall."

"It does not look difficult," my confident companion boasted.

"All right, but go quickly. Get on a step and grab the handrail. Ready?"

Instead of going quickly, Richard hesitated, holding his foot above the step to gauge the speed.

"Go!" I shouted.

He put his weight on a step. His lower half followed the step upward, but his top half remained motionless at the bottom of the escalator.

"Grab the handrail!"

Fortunately he grabbed the handrail at the last moment before he was bent in half at the waist. I managed to get a hand in the middle of his back and shoved his upper half into alignment with his rapidly ascending legs. Disaster was averted. A huge smile crossed Richard's face as he looked back at me.

"Richard, turn around and pay attention!"

I realized the worst was not over. I had to teach Richard how to get off the escalator in the next ten seconds!

"*Joie de vivre!* What an invention! How high up are we going?"

"Richard, stop talking. This is important. Listen to me. When we reach the top you must quickly STEP OFF. Literally JUMP OFF the end. Do you understand?"

"*Oui*," he responded, though it failed to give me any confidence of a successful exit.

When we reached the top he jumped a couple of feet and landed moving forward, more like a jogger than a business person, but at least he avoided making a human pile-up at the top of the escalator.

Success! But now I needed a break. When I saw a Bank of America branch office on the floor, I decided to give Richard a mini-tour of a modern financial institution. I thought it would also give me an opportunity to complete our discussion about money.

"Richard, I want to show you a modern bank. Follow me. This is a branch office of the largest bank in the United States. This little bank serves primarily the people who work in this building. There are many similar branches throughout the city, each serving small communities of people. In addition, there are many other banks competing against this banking company."

"It has a teller line, the same as our banks! Can we go in?" Richard said in a pitched voice out of character with his formal manner.

"Yes, but keep your voice down," I cautioned.

Turning his head from side to side like he was watching a tennis match, Richard said, "Are all these pictures of bank services?"

"Well, they sell all sorts of banking products and they want to tell their customers about what they offer."

"Could I buy a letter of credit?"

"I am sure you could. This brings up a topic I want your opinion on. I said earlier that money, in my opinion, is like a letter of credit. Money is a method to transport value earned. For instance, if I sold you my crop of grain in Walla Walla—"

"What are you saying?"

"Walla Walla is a city on the other side of the mountains. I was saying that if I was a farmer from Walla Walla and wanted to buy clothes from a store in Bellevue, a city on this side of the mountains, it would be much easier if I didn't have to carry my grain across the mountains, but could use a placeholder: money, in this instance. Do you agree with that?"

"Agreed. That is why I say that money begins as a product."

"So you agree that money is a transfer system to substitute for carrying around the products we produce when we want to go shopping. The important point is that money can only substitute, as you say, for a 'product' or, as I say, for 'earnings'. Is that right?"

"*Oui.*"

"You have not received much credit for this idea by the economists that followed you. In fact, the idea of money based on a product is lost. Most economists today think of money as wealth, just like the economists that preceded you. All of the major economic schools—Keynesian, Austrian, Classical— parrot the idea of money as wealth."

Richard replied, "It is really not an idea. It is a statement of fact. Knowing how money operates in an economic system is critical. When kings or princes try to obtain wealth through money they have forgotten that it all begins with a product."

Questioning my easily distracted listener as he walked around the bank was difficult, but I persisted. "I think I know the answer, but let me pose this question to confirm my suspicions. Is it correct that money creation should occur with the creation of a product?"

Richard lowered his eyebrows, but the corners of his mouth curled slightly in a nascent smile. He spoke emphatically: "*Oui.*"

"Does that mean it would be wrong for a central bank to create new money and put it into the banking system during a downturn when there are no new products?"

"Absolutely. That is exactly what happened with the Mississippi Company and in the South Sea Bubble. In France it was the central bank and in England it was the central government, but in both cases they doubled the available money in the belief that more money creates more wealth. In the case of these two companies the new money was in stock certificates backed by the government. These are perfect examples of buying an investment, such as stock certificates, in a company with no assets."

"Let me clarify: when you say 'no assets', you mean you are buying something that is not a wealth making mechanism as is, say, a purchase of jewelry. Is that right?"

"*Oui*, like you say, money is a concept. Both of those companies were concepts; there was no profit making capability. People bought a dream, a fantasy, a phantom, a *beau geste*: a terrible investment. You cannot imagine the euphoria felt by so many people who got their shares early on and they went up 20% in a week. I tried to explain the difference between speculation and investment, but no one listened."

Remembering Richard's windfall, I asked, "You 'took your money' out after your stake grew over a thousand percent. Why wasn't that an investment?"

Richard replied, "Ah, you noticed. I did not say 'wealth', because until I found a home for my money that turned a profit each year, it was only money looking to become an asset. Wealth and assets are equivalent. Wealth and money are not. Like you say, money is a method to move or convert wealth from one asset into another. As you move your money around you may have some speculative returns, but those are not investments because they likely will not reoccur."

"Let me make sure I understand the larger implication, Richard. You're saying that when governments create money out of the blue they're creating inflationary bubbles. When governments allow banks to expand the money supply by lending to new businesses they're facilitating the expansion of wealth. The first method is unwise because it creates more money without the creation of a proportional quantity of wealth. The second method is valid because it balances money creation with wealth creation. As you wrote, money comes after the product, so a government that creates money first has its monetary policy inside-out. The problem with that approach is inflation. Do I have that right?"

Richard gleefully chuckled and clapped his hands, mocking me. "Excellent. But I am not a teacher, just a simple banker. As a banker I understand the importance of stability. Stability provides the foundation of an economy. A pile of paper money is a weak foundation. A stack of gold bars is stronger, but unstable. A country with a solid job market is anchored to bedrock. An economy is not built on the number of paper bills circulating, but the number and diversity of wealth making mechanisms. Wealth making mechanisms are the economic engines of job creation."

"Thanks for the lesson!"

While Richard looked into a display case of old bills in the reception area, I reconsidered what I had just learned. *He offers some intriguing insights into how our modern monetary policy may be missing the mark. I should be able to recall the idea of turning money into wealth by picturing the escalator incident in an old bank office. The idea that wealth-creating mechanisms is the goal a central bank should pursue, rather than interest rate control, represents a major step up, from money creation to business creation. He again puts the focus on the entrepreneur rather than the regulator. I also like his definition of wealth as a mechanism that returns a profit, period after period. I can see how this perspective led him to sell his shares in the Mississippi Company while others held on through to bankruptcy.*

True Wealth

"Okay," I said, "but explain to me what you mean when you say 'wealth is the ability to consume'."

We had circumnavigated the bank floor and returned to the entry door. As we walked into the corridor outside the bank, Richard replied, "Wealth gives you the ability to consume because it generates a profit that you can spend year after year. Money kept in a drawer will only last a short time before it is gone. No one spends their last dollar. We only spend if we know more money is coming in. Money does not give you the ability to consume, but only the ability to worry."

"Many of the people in this building are in the 'wealth creation' business," I informed my Irish companion.

"That is a good thing. I am impressed that the business has grown so large."

"You really started something. Do you know that you have quite a legacy? Adam Smith mentioned you in 1776 as a source of his inspiration. Adam Smith is now the acknowledged Father of Economics."

"Roll up my leggings! That is impressive. I would never have imagined. I was just trying to explain why things work the way they do."

As I began to tell Richard about his legacy, I was struck by his genuine unfamiliarity with his fame. "You are regarded as the Father of Theoretical Economics."

"That is very humbling," Richard said, his eyes glistening. He turned away and looked over the railing down to watch the people silently rushing back and forth across the heavily carpeted lobby.

I walked up beside Richard and joined him in gazing at the floors below us. "You are a major figure in economics, but your theories took some time to gain acceptance, and were appreciated in the 18th century by only a small group of economist. Let me bring you back to reality. Although you are recognized as the first theorist, many of your ideas were misunderstood or ignored for years." Richard stretched his shoulders and put his thumbs under the collar of his coat and straightened his lapels.

He said, "Economics is a difficult science to swallow. What ideas were tough to digest? Give me an example of an idea I had that people found problematic?" He lifted up his chest in an exaggerated pose of defiance.

"Well, the one we were just talking about, your definition of wealth as the ability to consume."

Puzzled, Richard asked, "Why do you think that idea was questioned?"

Here was the opening I was looking for. "The primary reason is that your definition of wealth elevates the importance of profit. Profit today is considered the ugly sister of business. She's an integral part of the family, but she isn't very pretty, and she doesn't receive the respect one would expect."

"Peter, I can see that *you* believe that is wrong, but I cannot understand why anyone would think profit is not important. Profit is surplus money above the cost of production. Without a surplus, a seller and a buyer are just exchanging one product for another. For the economic system to expand each party must make a profit on each transaction. When the purchase price of a product is more than the cost to manufacture it, or the buyer of a product can resell a product for a higher price, these are wealth-making transactions. The profit concept makes the business system work. Regardless of government's perspective, money has a relatively minor role in creating wealth."

"By stating that money begins with a product, you created the standard view that trade builds wealth when product purchases occur," I added.

"Each exchange becomes part of a profit making activity," Richard elaborated. "In other words, an activity that does not generate a profit will not create wealth. This is the reason Louis XIV with all his expenditures could not make France wealthy. He spent extravagantly, much to the delight of his court, but none of his expenditures turned into a product that produced an income stream in his lifetime. His expenditures were just fireworks. Thrilled the crowd, but put nothing in their back pocket. So he just got progressively poorer and poorer in the world's most expensive palace."

"That's a great analogy."

"Understanding profitmaking also provides a definition for an asset, a product producing mechanism that repeatedly generates a profit. Therefore, a farm, a factory, and a law degree are each assets and, consequently, wealth. A gold coin, a diamond, and a royal title are neither profit making nor wealth. These baubles are a type of money looking for a profit making opportunity or a particular product – an object of desire – but not wealth."

"So Louis XIV was not wealthy," I offered. "He was just a boy with a lot of toys. His understanding of wealth doomed his country to financial collapse."

Richard nodded his head in appreciation, and his positive reaction refueled me. I charged on: "Unfortunately, the importance of growing wealth through products and services never fully entered into the realm of economic theories. Even today, people criticize companies for making profits, but it is the continuing stream of profits that allows a business to survive and grow. Job security depends on profits. A majority of people still believe wealth can be created through government spending, which I suspect is a great disappointment to you."

Richard shook his head in frustration. "Of all my ideas, I wanted to make it clear that government spending is always negative. Government spending is consumption. There is no buildup of assets to produce profits or investment. Government only purchases products to fulfill needs. Needs should be filled by profit-making firms to strengthen and sustain a society. Any potentially profitable niche filled by a government agency is a lost opportunity to build societal wealth."

"But people want free stuff. They see government as the way to obtain free stuff," I said.

"Do they not understand that it is their tax money that pays for government stuff? Ask them if they want to spend their money themselves, or if they want government to spend their money."

I suggested another explanation. "People see government expenditures as primarily for bridges, roads and schools."

"That is quite a change for me. Roads and bridges were always constructed by the landowners of the pastures and streams they crossed over. Granted, they charged a toll, but that was only paid by the people who used the roads and bridges. Usually, the person paying was a merchant transporting products to a market or a faire, while local people got free access."

Richard turned away from me to watch a woman in a tight pencil skirt, her knees rubbing together, strut into the bank. His distraction put our discussion on hold. "That is a very attractive style of clothing. You are a lucky man to be living in this era!"

Seeking relief from our dead-end discussion about government, I said, "Well, with that dose of reality, let's take a ride to the top of this building. Follow me around the corner. We are going to take an elevator. An elevator is a box that is lifted by cables to the top of the building. See that door opening? Come on."

Richard stepped into the elevator and I followed him. "Peter, the door is closing!"

"Don't move! Stay inside with me! After the door closes I will push a button and we will be taken to the 73rd floor and the Sky View observatory. You will feel the floor lift us in a second," I warned him.

"Oooh, are we moving up as fast as it feels?"

"Probably." About twenty seconds later the elevator door opened. We stepped out to a view above the Seattle skyline.

"Are we on top of the building?" Richard asked.

"Not quite. There are two floors above us with a restaurant and meeting rooms, but the view is not much better than on this floor. Let's go over to the windows and I'll point out the Merchant's Café where we had lunch."

Before I could orient him, Richard was peppering me with questions. "What is that big body of water? What is that big road? What is that orange ship on the water? What are those buildings? Where is the Smith Tower we passed walking up here? Is it safe to touch the window like that little girl is doing? How long can we stay here?"

"Slow down, Richard, and I will answer your questions one at a time. Now what's your first question?"

"Is that a mountain off in the distance over there?"

"Yes, that is Mt. Rainier, the tallest mountain in the state. It was named by the first English explorer to see this area, Captain George Vancouver. He named the mountain in 1792 for another captain in the British Navy."

"The Brits were here?" Not waiting for an answer, Richard moved south along the window wall. "What are those strange looking buildings directly below us?"

"Those are the sports stadiums for the Seahawks and the Mariners."

"What type of sports do they engage in? Like the Romans or the Greeks?"

"Neither – they play modern games with a ball they throw or hit."

"That sounds dull."

"There is much more than that to these games. Maybe someday we can go to a game," I suggested.

Richard's eyes widened and he looked at me like a friend. "I would like that." His comment almost produced tears in my eyes, and I thought about what an honor it would be to sit at a game with this respected economist and extraordinarily successful businessman, as his friend. It would be like sitting down with Warren Buffet or Bill Gates, or both.

Richard moved farther along. "What is that broad road that goes off into the distance toward Mt.

Rainier? Are those things moving on the roads trams? I have never seen them, but I know the Scottish coal mines have something that works like that."

"The road is called I-5 and it goes from Canada to our north all the way to the southern end of California and the Mexican border."

"Mexico and Canada I know, but what is California?"

"California is a state in our country, like County Cork in Ireland."

"Please, explain to me how those things move on the road without horses?"

"They are cars and trucks with a motor that propels them forward. A motor is a device that burns a type of oil and rotates the wheels."

"Fascinating, I would like to look more closely at them. Yet, I must acknowledge, I was more interested in the females I saw walking around in their spike shoes. I can't understand how they stay upright and even walk uphill."

"Do you have a shoe fetish?" I asked facetiously.

"What is that? Those shoes certainly fascinate me. Maybe that is what they are intended to do. Before I went to France to work in my cousin's bank I did not own a pair of shoes. Learning to spend a day in shoes and toughen up the tops of my feet was one of the most difficult things I ever did."

"Why did you need to toughen up the tops of your feet? If I ever have any problems with shoes it is the sides of the toes or heels that blister, not the tops."

"My problem wasn't blisters. The soles and toes of my feet were rock solid from growing up without shoes, but the stiff leather uppers cut the top of my feet terribly. I nearly bled to death the first couple of months until my flesh toughened up. I am impressed by the advances your cobblers have made in shoe design. You should be very proud of your country's accomplishments."

"Actually, the Italians are the world's best shoe manufacturers."

"*Joie de vivre*, I bought shoes for my wife in Florence..." Turning around and walking north to see if he had missed anything, Richard said, "Tell me about this body of water and what those large orange structures are below us, next to the water."

"You are looking at the Seattle harbor front. Those large orange structures are cranes used to load ships. The body of water is Puget Sound, a saltwater bay, connected to the Pacific Ocean. Most of the trade from this port is with Japan and China."

I decided to ask Richard for some advice. "The United States has a problem in trading with China. Labor costs are so low in China that they can produce almost any product at a lower cost than we can. Consequently, our manufacturers are going out of business. What would you suggest?"

"Labor costs are just one part of the cost of a product. If someone looked carefully into the situation, I suspect they would find that Chinese costs for packaging, shipping, and customizing the product for your country would significantly reduce the difference in overall labor costs. When I was in France we faced a similar dilemma, and the problem ended up being French taxes and French regulations and not foreign wage levels."

His answer surprised me so I inquired further, "You oppose regulation and accuse it of impoverishing the citizenry, is that correct?"

"I do not oppose regulation *per se*, but oppose regulation that is solely for the purpose of filling government coffers. Whereas regulation that forbids hunting or logging enhances a country. Misuse of regulation is one of a group of things government does that takes wealth away from the average citizen. The others are government debt that must be repaid by the citizenry, and of course taxation, which is abused in every country. The last, but most prevalent abuse of government power is expenditures for unnecessary and counter-productive activities such as war."

"Do you believe government abuses the power it wields?"

"In my time, the entire democratic movement was concentrated on stripping government of its abusive power. It appears from your statements that the movement was not successful."

I thought I needed to correct that unbecoming impression. "The United States was one of the first modern nations founded on democratic principles."

I decided a change of venue was in order. "Let's end this discussion. I want to show you one of the great business success stories of my hometown."

As we began our exit from Columbia Center I reviewed our recent conversation.

The view from the Observatory gave us a great view of the harbor and the ships engaged in trade. Richard made the point that the justification for trade is profit. Both parties in foreign trade must make money. Why do we as a country struggle with the policy of increasing trade when additional profit making obviously benefits everyone? Brilliant! I am amazed that so many of his ideas did not find their way through history.

Government spending does not create wealth. Of course it doesn't. Government spending doesn't go for new factories.

I quickly reviewed these observations in my mind as we descended the elevator. Richard rode down staring at his feet with his arms spread out in the corner to brace.

Customer Focus

When we walked out of the building, Richard discovered the streets were full of cars. I answered numerous questions, and eventually managed to get him headed toward our next destination, down the hill in route to First Avenue. At the bottom of the hill we turned right into a large brick plaza fronting the Federal Building. I directed Richard to a seating area south of the building.

"I need to drop off some paperwork. It will take only a minute. Will you wait here for me?" I asked. Richard acknowledged that he would.

I pushed through the bomb-proof stainless steel door, took two steps up to the security table, and dropped my keys and loose change into the plastic bowl adjacent to the metal detector. I put the bowl on the moving belt, walked through the radiation arch, I collected my keys and coins from the belt in a handful that I stuffed into a front coat pocket. Two diligent armed guards watched my every move like I was a sleight-of-hand magician. I continued my choreographed moves to avoid suspicion and strode quickly to the elevator bank. I pushed the button for the 32nd floor.

The IRS offices are only a couple of blocks from the waterfront and command gorgeous views of Puget Sound and the Olympic Mountains. I hadn't been here in ten years and I was amazed at the changes. Gone were the flimsy gray fabric covered panel system walls. The new cubicle forest was a stunning system with glass panels for every office, definitely top of the line.

This was an expenditure made during the Great Recession to stimulate the economy! Government economists argued that such expenditures boosted societal wealth with new office furniture. A federal agency gets first class furniture and at the same time the economy gets a kick out of the doldrums! Did the economy really work that way? Did borrowing money you could not afford really stimulate the economy? Sure, the panel company made a little money and the new walls certainly improved the attitude of the IRS employees, but was that the kind of prick that startled an economy into motion? Or does it work like Richard said, only when wealth-creating mechanisms are added? Are new businesses the way to increase employment and provide a steady repetitive monetary push with new profits and expanded employment? Is purchasing a product equivalent to building a factory?

I returned from my errand with some apprehension about whether my mysterious companion would be waiting for me, but was delighted to see him sitting exactly where I left him.

"Hey, Richard, do you like coffee?"

"I love it. I began drinking it in Paris at *Le Procope* and at the birthplace of ship insurance in London, Lloyd's Coffee House. Is coffee popular in Seattle?"

"Somewhat. I want to take you to a coffee shop that grew into one of the largest businesses in the world. They even have stores in China. The company is a chain of coffee shops called Starbucks. Their first store opened here in Seattle. Let's walk down to where it all began. It is about ten blocks away in our downtown market. Would you like to do that?"

"*Avec plaisir!*"

As we walked along First Avenue I told Richard the story of Starbucks. "Howard Schultz is the most famous entrepreneur associated with the company, although he did not start the firm. He is the person that made the company successful. Howard bought the company when it had just six stores, but twenty years after he took the helm, the company had over 17,000 stores, 200,000 employees, and locations in 61 countries."

"Magnifico, a real entrepreneur."

"He did well, but the business did not just perk along; it brewed some bitter results at first. Sensing disaster, Howard stepped up to counter the trend and restore his business. Sorry for the puns."

"I actually liked your use of the verb 'restored'. Is that where he put the focus, on the stores?"

"To a degree. Like most successful entrepreneurs he correctly put the focus on the customer. Howard realized the company had put its corporate goal of growth ahead of the customer experience. He moved to improve the customer experience by closing bad locations, retraining baristas, and strengthening the emotional attachment of the customer to the brand."

Richard noted, "You are pointing out one of the main differences between the business sector and the political sector. The political sector wants you to follow its desires and the business sector wants to fulfill your desires. Many people, when they analyze a business, look at how it is structured to make a profit. Business success is much more complicated. A successful business must first find a product or service not already offered, price it so a customer is satisfied, and then efficiently deliver it."

"Richard, that's the same approach Howard Schultz used to restore his business. First, he retrained his staff to ensure his product's quality met customer expectations. In February 2008 he closed all of his stores for half a day to reeducate all his baristas in how to brew the perfect coffee drink. He invested in new equipment to speed ordering and check-out. And to enhance the core values of his business the company spent $30 million to send 10,000 store managers to New Orleans to help the victims of a huge hurricane."

"Howard must be a man who understands the importance of giving an identity to a company and maintaining it through company activities. Does he have an explicit set of principles that guide his actions?"

"Yes, I've read about them, and while I can't recite them all, I can recall a few. My favorite is 'don't embrace the status quo.' From my perspective that's the soul of entrepreneurship: an insatiable desire to find a better way."

Relaxing his shoulders and taking his hands out of his pockets, Richard affirmed, "Ah, I agree that the drive to improve is the key to entrepreneurial success."

I said, "Another principle I admire is to innovate around the core. Many businesses chase the newest trend and don't focus on improving what they do best. Of course, the fashion industry lives on trends, but their trends are of their own making."

"In my time," Richard said, "fashion was how people indicated their place in society. Fashion became the new craze. It was not who you knew, but how you looked. Fashion influenced how people judged you. New clothes in the accepted style became a necessary expense."

"Fashion is big today."

Richard commented, "Fashion moved out of the dress shops into people's homes during the 18th century. Many large landowners covered their walls with fashionable art and tapestries. Sculptures were highly prized since that was the fashion of the Romans and Greeks. Many people traveled to obtain the latest and most prized art. I went to Italy myself to acquire a few pieces and personally accompanied them back since robbery was a constant hazard on the roads."

"What did you collect?"

"Mostly historical scenes. I like to see how things were done in the past. How people farmed or sold goods in markets. You can learn from the past."

Richard returned to his discourse on fashion. "Besides demonstrating their class, people used fashion to display their wealth and success. This was not a trend the French created. Historically, many societies followed this path. During my time women wrapped themselves in the most *chic* fabrics, but sacrificed comfort to display their attributes in an idealized way. Women wore corsets to reduce their waists to the size of a young girl's, and squeezed their breasts out the top of their corsets to form nice round lumps for men to ogle. As Shakespeare said, beauty is in the eye of the beholder. To complete the ensemble women inserted a farthingale beneath their skirts so that they ballooned out in a perfect cone shape to mirror the smaller cone shape of the corset. It was a very pleasing style to this man's eye."

"So shoes are not the only thing about women that attracts your attention!"

"Ah, Peter, consider this comment from Voltaire: 'All the reasoning of men are not worth one sentiment from a woman.'"

"*Touché*, you put me in my place. Go on with your history of fashion."

"Men were not immune from vanity. Most professional men wore tri-cornered hats, usually black. That was the only item of clothing that didn't require a sacrifice. Coats were made of wool with long tails that dragged in the snow in the winter and irritated you with their suffocating warmth in the summer. The style required that the sleeves were so tight you could not move your arms comfortably.

"It made you jealous of the scarecrows in the fields, with their freely swinging arms. It felt like you were being held in position by a suit of armor. Then the great disgrace of all was lace fringe escaping at the end of sleeves and around your neck. Ridiculous, but it was the fashion."

"It sounds like the fashions did not always fit your personal style."

As we passed the Sanitary Market entrance at the newspaper stand, I pointed across the street and directed Richard to continue up First Avenue. This way, we miss the crowds clogging the standard entrance. We walked north and crossed Pike Street, on our way to another entrance.

As we passed the flower stand on the corner, Richard said, "Look at these flowers. They are a fashion statement. The different varieties of flowers you bring into your house tell your visitors something about you. Remember that the Dutch in the middle of the 17th century valued some tulip bulbs more than precious gems? At the peak of the tulip craze people would risk their annual salary on a single bulb. This craze was driven solely by fashion speculation. The investment did not make any financial sense. Each bulb took a year to reproduce and it took many years before you could get multiple bulbs from a single bulb. Why did people think their single bulb would increase in value? Because fashion said it would? They believed that it did not matter how much they paid, for they could always sell at a higher price. *Au contraire*. If only speculation was so predictable."

I said, "Many of our greatest entrepreneurs have used fashion to distinguish their products from the competition, just like the ladies of your day. Steve Jobs, of Apple, used design to surpass his competition. Likewise, Howard Schultz of Starbucks utilized fashion, or style, actually, to make his stores stand out. He used a warm, inviting sitting room ambience to carry his customers away from the non-stop commercial environment outside. Starbucks is a place where people can take a moment to relax and enjoy one of the great pleasures of living in this international world. He's made his customers feel special, like a lady in a gorgeous gown displaying a perfectly shaped body in your time."

"I hope you are not saying he has made a cup of coffee the equal of a beautiful woman," teased Richard.

"Mr. Schultz achieved something much more modest. By turning Starbucks into a place to savor a tropical beverage on a cold misty afternoon in a temperate climate, he created a cozy place that made people feel good."

We looked in the windows of the coffee shop as we approached along the sidewalk. "This is it. What do you think?"

"*Bellissimo*, it looks like an Italian coffee bistro, but with *cachet*," Richard noted.

"Will you join me in a cup of java?"

Richard smiled. "Gladly."

I opened the door into the historic location and announced, "Welcome to Starbucks. Let's order drinks and then we'll find a seat. This place is unique in many ways! There is a specific technique used to order in Starbucks. First, get in line, read the menu, and decide what you want to drink. Then I will help you order."

Richard began to read the menu behind the counter. "Oh, they have tea. I will get tea."

"Good start, but now you need to decide if you want your tea hot or cold and what size."

"Hot tea of course, in a cup."

"All right, so your order so far is 'For here, hot tall Tazo'. Next, you need to select the kind of tea you want, green or black. You probably want black. It has more flavor. The barista, the women taking your order, also needs to know what kind of sweetener for your tea."

"I just want some sugar."

"We are getting there. Your order at this point is 'For here, hot tall Tazo black tea with classic'. Do you want any milk in your tea?"

"Milk would be good. I would like it half milk."

"What kind of milk do you want: soy, half 'n' half, non-fat, 1%, 2%, or whole?"

"I do not know what that means?"

"It is the amount of butter fat in the milk."

Baffled by the choices, Richard declared, "You choose. I have no idea."

We reached the counter and I ended my fun with Richard and placed our orders. "For here, one tall black Tazo 1% with classic, a Quad Grande 2% no-whip 170 mocha macchiato, and two croissants."

"What did you order to drink?"

"I ordered a 170-degree hot coffee with chocolate and 2% milk with four shots of espresso and the last shot on top of the drink, without whip cream and in a Grande size cup. Did you get all that?"

Richard just gave me a blank stare. I said, "I will give you a taste when it is ready. Move over here and our drinks will be placed on this counter. Listen closely. The Barista will call out your drink when she places it on the counter."

Our drinks and croissants arrived after a minute and we found large comfy chairs near the windows overlooking the street. Richard tried my drink and decided he preferred his tea. He told me he once had an espresso in Rome that was similar to my drink.

"Richard, would you like to know what economic idea you are given the most credit for?"

"Yes, that would be interesting."

Economic Growth

"Richard, I think this may surprise you. When economists who came after you talk about your contributions to the study of economics they point to your recognition of the importance of the entrepreneur."

"That is startling! I would have thought my explanation about how all wealth originates from land ownership would be the important concept. When I wrote about the role of entrepreneurs it was just to explain how monetary growth should occur."

"Today," I explained, "monetary growth is the important topic since it's seen as the source of new jobs by Keynesian economists and as the source of inflation by Austrian School economists. Attempts to reconcile these distinctly different views have tied our monetary policy into a knot."

"The wealthy, influential, and powerful in my time regarded the activities of their class as far more important than the activities of clever, original, and innovative business people. Business skills were not appreciated. They were simply seen as the normal tools of the businessman, like any craftsman's abilities. I am very pleased that entrepreneurship is now recognized as a special skill."

"I'm glad you're pleased, but your elevation of the entrepreneur hasn't made them the lead characters in the economic theatre. In fact, the entrepreneur has a secondary role today. National governments and to some extent academic economists direct the economic show, and play the biggest roles. Using incentives and disincentives, they move and shuffle about the various other economic actors to adjust the economic drama to their vision. This is most apparent in the economic policy and regulation pursued by the federal government."

"How can an agency that knows nothing about business processes gain directorial control over business activities?" blurted Richard, obviously frustrated. "That makes no sense to me. Government has no knowledge of what entrepreneurs and businesses need to grow and strengthen. How did that happen?"

"Governments control the national purse. Their ability to tax and regulate allows them to influence the market. All political parties want to redirect the course of business growth into areas of interest to their political membership." I paused to take a large bite out of my croissant.

"I despise the power that taxation gives to government. At least I was right to fear that trend," Richard admitted. "These croissants look like real French creations!

"Peter, you must be working on some idea on how to reverse that taxing direction," Richard said, challenging me. He reached down for his croissant and eased back in his chair like he was expecting a long explanation.

"Well, my main strategy is to get your idea about the importance of the entrepreneur on to bookshelves. I will stress that principle in my Cantillon book. I, like you, believe that 'big government' is bad.

"One of the issues I see is that it is impossible for people in government to avoid consideration of their personal interests when managing public resources. Often this involves avoiding stress in their life by not opposing excessive costs presented by contractors, or by not objecting to changes requested by special interest groups, or by not keeping salaries under control. Why go through the hassle of objecting? No one likes conflict and consequently there are usually few critical eyes overseeing a public official's duties.

"I think the simplest way to overcome this dilemma is to reduce government to essential security and police functions. Can the core services typically provided by a corps of government workers be accomplished by the business community?" I wanted to challenge Richard to take a position and at the same time create a moment to finish eating my croissant.

Richard responded, "That idea is not far-fetched. In my time most of the infrastructure–bridges, roads, dams, irrigation projects–were constructed by wealthy landowners and not by the government. Even the armies were largely resident militias assembled, trained, and deployed by local lords. If infrastructure in my day was provided by unsophisticated farmers, then surely your highly advanced construction firms today could build the roads and bridges according to standards set by industry.

"I can see how government could be left out of the equation or have a much smaller role. Since the projects are built by the private sector why interject a government manager? You could turn road construction over to a subsidized utility like the water and sewer system. This would reduce overhead costs, which are non-productive expenses."

Richard had the look of someone chasing an idea around in his mind. "Government began as a system to protect the kings and sultans, not the farmers. Everyone else was expected to defend himself, but protection of the 'King' was a community effort. That was government's only responsibility. In fact, government was created solely to protect the King and the King's possessions. At a time when common people were considered the King's possessions, they received some protection, but that was secondary. Government in my time was not organized to protect common people."

"That's an original viewpoint."

"What you are suggesting in regard to work is not too different from the situation when I lived in Paris. All young craftspeople had to work an unpaid apprenticeship. They received lodging and food in compensation for the work they accomplished during their training. Soldiers joined the military for the adventure, a uniform, and a meal, but little hope of getting paid. Everyone received just a bit more than subsistence pay until they were accomplished and valuable employees. This was not a bad system. Everyone found a way to survive, even if not in luxury, and at the end of their apprenticeships they emerged as trained craftspeople, each person to their manor born."

I ignored Richard's reference to life being preordained by birthright and returned to our earlier conversation about his idea that 'wealth is the ability to consume'. "Richard, if we took wealth creation as a basic principle for organizing society, how would that alter what we do today?"

"Ah, think of the approach as the difference between a hog farm and a vault full of gold equal to the value of the farm. Most people and most countries would prefer to own the vault of gold bars. Why, they would not have to work to extract the gold, and they still have immense wealth to consume. The point they are missing is the amount of gold in the vault is limited. The hog farm will continue to produce virtually forever and provide jobs every year.

"Money and wealth are different. A hog farm is wealth. Each year it produces hogs for the market that can be sold for money. Wealth making mechanisms and a hog farm are like a money tree compared to a stack of gold. Initially, they may be valued equally, but the money tree will keep producing year after year. Which would you rather have?"

It seemed as though Richard was about to launch into an extended explanation, so I settled into the Starbucks experience. I cradled my bowl of coffee, inhaled its dark musky essence, and answered, "Oink, oink, hog farm, of course."

"If you are going to write a book about my ideas please keep animal sounds out of it, but you should begin with that concept of wealth. Understanding that the resources of a country should be directed toward wealth creation is paramount. The basic resource is the people resource. The people resource should be nurtured to produce entrepreneurs because they provide the ideas and energy to create new industry and new employment opportunities. Economics begins with this fundamental goal: educating people who can create wealth generating mechanisms.

I had to ask, "What would happen to a country if the educators thought profit-making was evil and education was primarily for teaching people how to act?"

"What a horrible thought. The country would collapse as it would fail to provide sufficient income to support the populace. Over time people would get discouraged and abandon work as a meaningless activity. But don't despair earning money is not going away."

"Remember that the corset spawned an industry. The corset was manufactured from thin and strong silk fibers that came not from the country of manufacture, but came on the backs of camels from countries far, far away. Even the wooden stays first employed were soon replaced by stronger whale ribs, carved and shaped for such a trivial but economically important purpose. Do you think a King or Queen would have suggested whale bone for such a use? I think not. Only an entrepreneur has the focus and motivation to make such improvements. Only the entrepreneur can create new industries. I hope your country has learned that lesson."

"How can government encourage entrepreneurs?"

Richard finished his croissant, crinkled up the pastry wrapper, and cast it over his shoulder on to the floor. Fortunately, no one else saw his unacceptable behavior. I knew I would need to discretely pick up the discarded bundle upon our exit.

Richard responded to my question. "The French government established some precedents with respect to encouraging entrepreneurship. In 1466 King Louis XI declared his intention to foster a national silk industry in Lyon. Nothing much else happened for the next 100 years until King Francis I granted a royal charter to two entrepreneurs, Étienne Turquet and Barthélemy Naris, to create a silk trade, and gave monopoly manufacturing rights to Lyon. By the time I was born over 14,000 looms were operating there and more than a third of the population was supported by the industry. I am not suggesting that a monopoly is always necessary for the growth of an industry, but entrepreneurs certainly are. The lesson is that government cannot start an industry, but it can nurture one.

"Another approach is to enhance an entrepreneur's business idea through government patronage. The two largest French tapestry houses, Beauvais and Gobelins, both benefitted greatly from the patronage of King Louis XIV. His patronage allowed both houses to reach financial heights never equaled after his buying spree ended. When his financial difficulties forced him to reduce his purchases, both companies suffered critical financial losses. A 'sea change' is difficult to avoid after you have left the harbor.

"Another strategy the French government used that could be embraced by many countries is the adoption of policies to reduce the purchase of foreign goods. The French government constantly monitored when French gold was shipped across the border to purchase foreign goods. In response, it tried to persuade Swedish ironworkers, Dutch shipbuilders, and even Murano glassworkers to operate within the borders of France and thus reduce the outflow of gold to foreign lands. Essentially, the idea is to decrease imports and expand exports."

I volunteered, "We still deal with that issue today. So the Chinese are employing the right approach by helping American companies open factories in their country. Although a bigger problem is that our government borrows half its money from foreign investors and governments."

Richard's face contorted. "That is very bad. I am sure you are aware that at the end of my book I explain that money lent by foreign sources to a state is 'always burdensome and harmful'. This is one of those lessons that I had hoped would find a home in basic economic theory."

"It is an idea that did not resonate."

"Peter, why is that? It is such a simple and obvious concept."

"Well, politicians do not want to disappoint their followers. They ignore the economic consequences of borrowing. Their logic is that if government can repay the debt, it is acceptable to borrow. They do not consider the long term consequences. They are concerned with the short term consequences of providing a new road or bridge, not the overall health of the economy."

"Part of being a leader is to have a long-term perspective," Richard insisted.

"I totally agree, and it's ironic, but I often think our politicians are not up to the task of being leaders."

Richard sat back in his comfy chair and asked, "What qualities do your politicians possess?"

I rubbed my forehead and responded somewhat hesitantly, "I suppose they're the qualities of being tall, good looking, and having the oratorical ability of a Baptist minister–traits no electorate can resist."

"Is an understanding of your economic system a consideration at all?"

"Not much."

"Your country is being managed by fools!" Richard said, leaning forward out of his seat.

"It is not that bad," I suggested, "because political influence on the economic system is diluted by many powerful market forces. Bank power resides in their expertise in selecting who has the opportunity to develop new business. It is these entrepreneurs who are the dominant societal influencers, and they support the banking system that gave them an opportunity to be successful. The press and media emphasize the politicians and their actions. People get a distorted view of who actually moves society."

"That is reassuring, but I want to see more of how your industry functions," Richard said. Clearly his attention was now focused elsewhere. "If you do not mind I would like to walk through your market to see what is for sale. That is a place that is familiar to me, and I would like to compare it to my time."

"No, I don't mind. Let's go."

We rose from our seats. I took a couple of steps sideways, smoothly scooped up his paper wrapper from the floor, and looked around for the recycling container. I felt good about the discussion over these last few minutes.

It will be easy to remember Richard's focus on the entrepreneur at Starbucks. He stressed the importance of the entrepreneur to economic growth. He even suggests privatization of infrastructure construction. His ideas are remarkably modern. His whole concept of a government focus on wealth creating mechanisms is both original and has the potential to make possible an economic leap forward. It is pleasant to imagine changing the focus of government from policing us to leading us in creative economy building.

Competition Pricing

As we left Starbucks I directed Richard to cross the alley. Pike Place Market's back door is directly across the street from the original Starbucks. Although the entire area is officially "the Market", the conventional street front stores like Starbucks do not have the ring of authenticity that permeates the main building with its long central corridor and stalls on either side. Starbucks is separated from this building by a roadway that was once a street, but now is more a pedestrian domain where cars are stopped by a flood of jaywalkers. People surge around the motionless vehicles the same way salmon swim around boulders in an Alaskan stream. We joined the crowd, dodged the stopped vehicles, and made our way into the Market.

At this end of the Market the vendors are mostly craftspeople who rent space by the day. We passed a couple of tables displaying jewelry, mostly earrings and bracelets. "Did women in your time wear earrings?" I asked Richard.

"They did in the last century, but now the style is to wear bonnets tied with a ribbon that covers their ears." Moving to the next table, Richard commented, "Now, women do wear bracelets. These bracelets are beautiful. The bracelets in my time also included precious stones, but colored enamels were equally popular."

As we continued up the clogged aisle we reached the tables occupied by the flower vendors. Richard was intrigued by the variety of flowers. I really got his attention when I explained that the flower merchants could provide flowers all year long by using greenhouses. Since he was now an expert on glass, he readily accepted my explanation.

Across from the flower vendors were tables covered with tie-dyed clothing. "Richard, take a look at these clothes. They are made using a technique called tie-dying. Fabric is bunched and tied in place to prevent color from reaching the inner parts of the fabric and then dipped in a colored dye. The result is that only part of the fabric is dyed. Then the artist dries the fabric and bunches it in a different way to expose other parts of the material and dips it again in another color of dye. This is repeated many times until the finished product looks like this. What do you think?"

"It is very colorful. What is this fabric?" he said as he reached out to feel the material. "It is very soft. I imagine this would be pleasant to wear. Is it popular?"

"It is made of cotton. Cotton is the most popular fabric for its low price and soft touch on the skin. I prefer to wear cotton whenever I can."

Richard smiled. "I thought it was cotton. This fabric from India is all the rage currently in Europe. Cotton is usually sold as a print from India called 'chintzes', very soft and a real favorite of the court. It is so popular that the fabric manufacturers in England and the Dutch Republics are asking their governments to ban its importation. I hope they fail, but they have immense influence. To compete fairly the manufacturers should just improve their fabric processing skills. Competing that way would advance the quality and variety of goods. If they come up with something exceptional, they could sell it back to the people of India."

We continued on past the jam, jelly, and nut vendors, which did not interest Richard. He did stop to look at the small animal sculptures made from volcanic ash, although I believe he was more interested in the volcanoes than the products made from the ash. He told me he had visited the volcanoes south of Rome.

The next show stopper was the fish merchant. Richard's interest was not the fish, but the ice that the fish were lying in. "What is this white material?" he asked reaching down to touch the bed of white snow surrounding the fish.

"It is manufactured ice. A company uses machinery to lower the temperature of fresh water until ice forms. Then they sell the ice to the fishmonger. The merchant is using the ice to keep his fish fresh and cold just like they came directly from the North Pacific."

"So this is manmade? Can I touch it?"

"Sure, go ahead, but the ice is cold so just take a small handful."

"Ooooh, it is very cold. Amazing! You have really made some dramatic scientific discoveries. I applaud your business people."

"Great, I'll pass on your congratulations, but as you can see our farmer's markets are probably very similar to yours. I'd like to show you something quite different."

"Before we leave," Richard inquired, "I want to know how the prices of goods are set. Are prices set by the state or by the businessman?"

"Prices are set by the owner of each stall. In the morning he evaluates how his sales went the previous day. If they were very good and reduced his inventory, he might decide to increase his prices to lower his volume of sales, but increase his profit on each item sold. This is not a simple decision since he wants to grow his profit. Higher prices might affect his sales to a point insufficient to make up the difference even with larger margins. Fewer sales with higher margins could mean lower overall profits."

"Peter, when you say 'fewer' and 'higher' and 'increase' and 'lower', that is an explanation that I understand, but it will not work for most of your readers. Do not use that language in a new book about my theories. Use an example, say, of a merchant selling crab, like the man in front of us. If he is going to change his crab price tomorrow, how does he go about it?"

"Sorry for the gobble-gook. Okay, let me start again. Imagine a young seafood merchant trying to figure out how to price his merchandise. He knows every other seafood merchant will compete on price, and selecting the right price will determine his sales and success in the fish business. He knows that proper pricing requires knowledge about how the consumer will respond to a certain price. Our young merchant suspects that a small price change will not change consumer behavior, but that may not be true. If crab is priced at $4.99 per pound, a price increase of even a penny might affect sales.

"Richard, the best way for him to proceed is to experiment, to try different levels of prices and determine what price provides the best outcome. Even a simple experiment of raising prices requires research. Our young merchant needs to go around and learn the prices his competitors are charging for their crab, then, evaluate those prices to determine his own price.

"He may discover one particular merchant has a sign with a specific price, but his salesmen are in the corridor outside his stall offering a 10% discount to potential customers. This creates an illusion in the customer's mind that they just happened to pass the stall at the opportune moment, and here is a bargain they should snap up. It also means the price of crab is not what is listed on the sign, but 10% less."

"Won't engaging in deception cause the other merchants to react to his practices?" Richard probed.

"Research by academics has shown that, surprisingly, there's a great deal of tolerance among competitors of 'creative' strategies to entice customers. If a technique works, the other merchants will quickly adopt it."

I continued my example. "So our young merchant returns to his stall and evaluates his results. He collected prices on not just crabs, but the other seafood that he sells – salmon, mussels, Manila clams, and halibut. When he looks at the prices he realizes they all vary. There is no uniformity in the pricing of any of the products he surveyed. So he looks at the lowest price of each of the products and discovers that the lowest prices are found not at one shop, but at different shops. He is baffled. What should he do? His calculations show that if he tries to match all of the lowest prices that he found, he would lose money on all of his products.

"He tries to figure out what is going on. Are his costs too high compared to the other merchants? He buys from many of the same suppliers as they do and after all, the law forbids wholesale suppliers from offering different prices to different retailers, so that could not be the case."

"Stop right there! There are laws requiring wholesalers to give all retailers the same price? Explain that, please."

"It's true. There is a group of regulations called antitrust laws that prohibit certain types of sales that restrain trade. For instance, a wholesaler cannot offer one merchant a price and offer a different price to another merchant for the identical product. In the case of seafood, few items are 'identical'–they vary in freshness, flavor, and place of origin. But certain products such as Manila clams or mussels are considered identical. From a practical standpoint, other products are usually offered at the same price by the wholesaler to avoid any antitrust complications. Of course, a wholesaler can offer a different price depending on the quantity purchased. So in consideration of his costs, our young merchant must be conscious of the quantities he buys."

"Interesting. Business is not simple, is it? Please proceed."

"The highly competitive price landscape our young merchant uncovered might result from a technique called a 'loss leader'. This is when a merchant lowers the price on one product to entice customers. The hope is that after they make a discounted purchase, customers will remain and make other purchases with higher margins.

"With that understanding, our young merchant can decide which prices to compete against. For instance, his sales of Manila clams may be relatively insignificant so he decides not to compete on price for sales of that product. On the other hand, his sales of crabs are the bulk of his business and he feels obligated to compete on the price of crabs to maintain his core market share. So he lowers his price per pound of crab to the lowest price offered by the other merchants.

"This decision substantially reduces his profit so after a week he goes back to the merchant with the low price on crab to see if the situation is the same. He finds the price of crab is now $2 per pound above his price, and the price of Manila clams is half his price. This is confusing to the young merchant because his crab sales didn't change much with the lower price.

"He quickly realizes his competitor is adjusting prices more often than he is. He also realizes there is more subtlety to pricing than he expected. Apparently, the customer retains the impression of a merchant offering lower prices even after the merchant raises prices. The customer does not shop on the basis of price on every shopping trip, but gets an impression about a merchant. The customer retains that impression until he has a different experience of the price structure with that particular merchant. Our young merchant takes in this knowledge and begins to develop a pricing strategy.

"On his way back to his stall he struggles anxiously through the Friday night crowd. He wants to get back quickly to serve the crowds surrounding his stall. When he finally reaches his stall the obvious strikes him. People are not going to shuffle back and forth to compare prices on a busy night, so he can raise prices during these times. He looks around and realizes that most of his customers come in through the side door of the market. He surmises that his customers are not comparing his prices with the low priced merchant at the other end of the market. His customers are probably evaluating his prices only against those of the merchant just around the corner. It occurs to him that, in fact, they may get their pricing information somewhere else altogether. He notices that many customers look at their cell phones before placing an order. Are they comparing his prices with prices on the Internet? Of course they are!"

"Good story, Peter. Prices are set today just like they were in my time. A merchant sets an initial price, but whether a product sells depends on the choices of customers. If customers refuse to purchase because prices seem too high, merchants must reduce prices to sell their products. The purchase process is a bit like a Dutch auction. The product stays unsold until the price drops enough to attract a customer. Both the merchant and the customer have a role in determining the selling price.

"By the way, what are cell phones?"

Consumer Pricing

"I will show you my cell phone as we walk up the hill to the bank, but first, since you asked, let me finish my explanation of pricing.

"The government has no direct role in setting the price of a product except for slightly increasing a product's cost by the amount of taxes associated with its production and regulation compliance. A merchant will set a high initial price to maximize his profit, but if no buyers step forward he will gradually reduce his price until the product sells. Products sell in our markets just as you state in your *Essai,* based 'on the desires and moods of men'. The 'desires and moods of men' vary greatly. On some days a merchant may make a huge profit and yet on the next day take a loss.

This process is based on the choices of consumers and not the cost to produce the product.

"Likewise, the quantity of a product in the marketplace does not determine the price a merchant sets. At the retail level, supply and demand play a small role. We still abide by your theory that price 'is settled by bargaining' between buyers and sellers. Many economists who follow this line of thinking discount the importance of supply and demand theory, and strongly support your thesis that market prices have 'no exact or geometrical foundation'. This same school of economists also agrees that inflation results from too little competition, and not some imbalance of the money supply and product demand. Basically, prices and sales are negotiated through the actions of buyers and sellers and are subject to their wants and not some mathematical equation."

"Peter, what is the name of this economic school that follows my pricing theory?"

"It is called Austrian economics and is based on a restatement of your theories in the 1870s by an Austrian economist named Carl Menger."

"It is very gratifying to hear that price settlement still occurs in the same manner as I described it nearly 300 years ago. In a way it is shocking. Other aspects of life have changed so dramatically and yet the foundation of business pricing remains unchanged. Prices are set by sellers and accepted or rejected by buyers. It is a negotiation, as I said, and not based on supply and demand like the Egyptians stated. Amazing!"

Richard stopped and stared into the distance, basking in the realization that he had been right. I stood back, not wanting to break his moment of victory. History had proven his theories correct and the realization stunned and humbled him. Most scientists get this satisfaction in their lifetime, but to have waited 300 years intensified the moment. Richard actually started to get a little unsteady with emotion; he took a couple of steps forward and leaned against one of the old cast iron columns that gave the Pike Place Market its authentic character. Now I was stunned. I waited for him to say something.

"Thank you, Peter. I am ready to go to the bank you want me to see. There is another lesson here. When everything is open and visible to all parties, fairness will prevail. The open and competitive marketplace cannot be replaced. Business understands the best deals are made in the open. 'All the world's a stage' and the best action occurs before an audience. I love the openness of your market."

"Richard, it occurs to me that you made another contribution to economic thought that will dramatically affect the future once I remind the public about it in my book."

"What is that?"

"Few people realize that pricing based on supply and demand is an ancient concept. The

Romans, Greeks and Egyptians all thought prices were established by a ratio of supply and demand. Your new idea of pricing as a process of bargaining based on the actions of the merchant, as I described for the crab vendor and the crab consumer, is a revolutionary transformation of supply and demand theory. Let's call it 'negotiated pricing', but it's really the idea of pricing being settled through the shopping process."

I took out my cell phone. Holding my cell phone cradled in both hands, I said, "Follow me out to the street and I will show you how this works."

Richard looked down at my iPhone. He seemed baffled by what he was looking at. I pushed the button to turn it on. "By swiping your finger across the bottom, like this, you can open it up and turn it on. See the picture of the sun with the word 'weather' underneath? You can touch it and get a weather forecast for the next six days. Watch me. I tap the sun symbol and get more information. Here, you try it."

Richard took the iPhone and tapped the sun symbol. "How does this thing change colors?"

"Since you do not know what electricity is and nothing about electronics, let me just say it happens because you ask it to change. Let me think for a second, so I can come up with a better explanation.

"When you are riding a horse and you shake the reins and shout 'giddy-up', the horse responds by changing its gait from a walk to a trot. The cell phone works the same way. When you push on it in a certain way it responds to your commands. Do you know what a chameleon is?"

Richard cradled the cell phone like a baby in his cupped hands. He said, "Is that the animal from the Americas that changes color?"

"Yes, exactly. A cell phone works in a similar way. When you push a certain spot it changes color in certain places and in different shapes. The sun on the top of the image is formed by the cell phone making part of its skin in a circular shape turn orange. It is that simple," I said, trying to resist a smile.

"The person that made this thing must be very rich."

"It was not one person that made this but thousands, all across the world, and some are very rich. Go ahead and push another spot. Try the picture of a flower."

Richard screamed, "What did I do? Is it broken? I did not touch anything."

"Calm down, Richard. It just shut down. Give it to me and I will resuscitate it!"

Richard handed over the phone and stared at my every action to see how I would restore life to the little black rectangle that he had just killed.

"All you need to do is push gently in this circular recess at the bottom of the screen." I pushed the button and the iPhone came back to life. "Do you remember how to activate it? Just swipe your finger across the bottom. Okay, there you are – back to the main screen. Here, you take the phone and find the picture of the flower and push it."

Although filled with fear and excitement in equal quantities, Richard managed to push the picture symbol and open my library of pictures. I showed him how to start a slideshow and page through the various pictures. He especially liked the video of my granddaughters playing in a small blow-up pool. The pictures of me on my tractor cutting down three foot high pasture grass also got big smiles.

Just then the traffic light changed. I grabbed Richard's sleeve and said, "Follow me." He never looked at me or where I was leading him. His eyes were glued to the small screen in his cupped hands. "Let's cross the street. I want to take you to this bank and show you the place where a famous financial bubble played out less than five years ago."

"How do I get back to the 'main screen', I think you call it?" Richard was paying attention only to his new toy.

"Just push the recessed button below the screen. Remember to swipe your finger and you will be back to the main screen." Richard followed my instructions like a pro. I figured I had lost him to the world of electronic gadgetry, so I just gently directed him up the three blocks to the old Washington Mutual headquarters building. He never looked up from the iPhone screen. He began to quiz me about his discoveries on the phone: "Do you know what time it is in London? Why is the Bluetooth on? Have you read the plot summary of the movie *Compulsion*?"

I decided it was time to recover my iPhone before he erased something. He didn't resist returning the phone, but he made me promise to let him look at (*play with*) it later.

Outside the bank I briefly explained how to use the large revolving doors then led Richard into the lobby. "Only a few years ago this was the lobby of a highly successful bank called Washington Mutual. It was named after the first president of the United States. The bank's expertise was making mortgage loans to homeowners. Do you know what a mortgage is?"

Richard gazed at the high ceiling and gave a somewhat practiced response. "I am very familiar with mortgage loans according to English common law. It is the right of a creditor to an interest in a debtor's property, and gives the creditor the right to sell the property in the event the debtor defaults.

"The thing I am not familiar with is the president. Why would a bank take the name of a judge?"

"I should have explained that president is the term we use to describe our highest ranking elected official. I know that during your time the term president referred to a high-ranking judge in the French judicial system. Washington was the very first president of our country and is highly respected for his honesty. He could never tell a lie. It was not a creative choice, but one that bank customers could easily remember.

"Mortgages also have a long history in our country. Some of the first European settlers, the pilgrims, brought the idea from England. Early on, mortgages required a 50% down payment and had a term of five years. Today, mortgages are typically for thirty years and require a 10% down payment. The financial terms of mortgages are set at a level that allows the maximum number of people to own a home. These levels are determined by government regulators."

"Uh oh, that is a problem," said Richard. "I agree that 'everybody must live', but that should occur through wages that provide sufficient income to live within society. When the government intervenes it will push the boundaries of what is financially possible. Am I right? Is that what happened?"

"Richard, you are impressive. That is exactly what happened. Regulators lowered lending standards until eventually so many people were in the mortgage pool, no one had room to swim. When the first person slipped under the water, everyone panicked and rushed to get out. There was no escape at that point, and more people got dragged below the surface and drowned. This shell of a bank was left holding their mortgages. We call this event the Great Recession, because the economy collapsed when the banks panicked and stopped lending."

"I suppose the banks got blamed," Richard said with a knowing smirk.

"Yes, but they were not blameless. They entered every niche that the regulators approved. They did not conduct adequate due diligence. They justified their actions by the fact that regulators allowed them to act, and the market enabled them to act since there was a slew of willing bond buyers to purchase mortgage loans.

"The federal government exacerbated the situation when they made laws requiring banks to make loans to marginal borrowers. The banks knew better, but kept pushing loans on unqualified borrowers. Surprisingly the regulators even made laws requiring banks to lend to many unqualified purchasers.

"Of course, it was not the regulators' money that was at risk—the money belonged to the bank depositors. Banks forgot that their depositors were their customers. Banks instead began looking to the regulators for direction and approval of their actions. A government housing agency, called HUD, replaced depositors as the strongest market influencer by setting required lending quotas for banks."

Richard shook his head in a knowing way. "It is human to look for someone to blame. What child who falls down on the playground was not pushed? What employee late for work was allowed to sleep in by a clock that did not wind itself? In my time we blamed the King or the banks, but never our own foolishness. It appears that tendency remains."

"Although we call this event the Great Recession, most commentators place the blame on an increase in housing prices. They genuinely believe the cause of the problem was a housing bubble."

Richard said, "Let me give you my opinion. Bubbles are something I have a bit of knowledge about. Can we go somewhere and sit down? I am uncomfortable standing in this magnificent lobby and just talking. I noticed the rain stopped as we were walking up the hill–can we go outside and watch the sun break through the clouds?"

"Certainly. It may involve taking an escalator or elevator since we entered on Fourth and need to descend to Third. Are you OK with that?"

"I would enjoy it."

"Follow me over here." I took Richard to an escalator that descended to the ground floor.

We went outside to a patio area with an attention grabbing stainless steel sculpture. We found a table placed along the building wall that was used as an outdoor lunch spot when the weather was good. The seats were dry so we sat down. Richard gave his attention to the sculpture, composed of four full sized stainless steel Doric columns. Two were upright, but the column segments were misaligned as if the columns had barely survived an earthquake. Two similar columns were toppled and laying on the ground. The capital from one of the columns was sticking out of the ground like it had fallen just a moment earlier and penetrated the patio floor. There was an archaeological feel, a sense of hallowed ground, to the sculpture court. The feeling was enhanced by the immense wall of the modern bank building that rose to the side, shielding this 'sacred' ground.

Richard was struck by the symbolism. "What an incredible irony to have these ancient building forms laying at the base of such a magnificent image of modern commerce and business."

"Yes, it looks as if the ancient foundations of commerce remain, although showing the ravages of time."

"It shows a respect for the ancient foundations of business," Richard commented, "the builders of this new edifice of industry leaving these early structures undisturbed."

"Richard, come over here." Placed on a low wall surrounding a fountain was a plaque. "Look, here is the name of the sculpture, *New Archetypes,* by Anne & Patrick Poirier. A piece by two French artists. See Richard, you are not the only French connection."

"I am happy to be linked to such great and meaningful art."

"*New Archetypes*? Are they saying the skyscraper, as we call these tall buildings, are the standard we judge our business success upon?" I asked.

Richard said, "I prefer to think we measure business success in terms of the wealth creating mechanisms that a company discovers. Often those wealth creating discoveries like the ingredients of steel come from beneath the land. Mining is a great source of wealth. For instance, Thomas Newcomen's development of the steam engine to pump water out of coal mines will enable mines to be dug in places never before accessible. Wealth is not the money made or glorified in a tall building, but the new mechanisms incorporated into an economy that sustain jobs and make new money year after year. This is the difference between money-making and wealth-creation that I explained to you back at the restaurant. Thomas Newcomen's wealth-creating machine will expand mining to new sites. His invention will employ many more men than the current system of the mining art could possibly achieve."

I said, "I am a great admirer of your ideas about money and wealth, but I would like to know a bit more about you. In the restaurant you said you were a fugitive. Could you explain that?"

Richard looked shocked, and he took a moment to respond. *Maybe I shouldn't have interrupted him while he was making the distinction between making money and wealth creation, but he did explain that earlier. I can certainly connect his idea of pricing based on a negotiation between buyer and seller with the Pike Street Market. It is also important to remember he rejects supply and demand as a primary pricing factor, as do I.*

Paper Money Legacy

We returned to the table. Richard looked up and down the street and then spoke to me in confidential tones, "I did not want to talk in a public lobby. This small sculpture park provides enough privacy for a personal conversation.

"In May 1734 I was living in London when my house burned to the ground. The authorities assumed I died in the fire, but the truth is I emerged from the fire in a bit of a daze. I have never been able to shake the daze, but I was able to resume my life. I left London and traveled to Suriname where I lived under the name Chevalier de Louvigny.

"People say death is mysterious. It really is. I am not sure if I died in Suriname or in London. I know the authorities are looking for me in both countries. Clearly, the trail has gone cold. Even now I do not know if I am alive or dead or a ghost. Feel my hands."

I reached across the small metal tabletop and grasped his hands. They felt slightly chilled but that may have been just from the cool spring air; to this novice ghost-buster they felt like the hands of a living man. I asked, "Do you think you are a reincarnation?"

"No, I am totally aware of my previous life. It is as clear as when I was living. The only difference is this time my life is not continuous. I have had numerous incidents like I am having in this city, but there are always gaps between occurrences."

"What was your last incident like?"

"I was in a library talking to an economist who was born after I left France."

"Who was that?"

"Jean Baptiste Say. Do you know of him?"

"Yes, he is a French economist who was born about 100 years after you. He wrote in the early 19th century. If I were to draw a history line through early economic theory that line would start with you and connect to Say. Your foundation concepts are consistent with one another. Was Say alive in his own time like I am, or in some space-time warp like you?"

Richard curled the left side of his mouth in a half smile as he realized that his situation baffled me as much as it had the other people he had encountered in his travels. I wondered if his hesitation indicated he was as confused about his existence as I was.

"If I remember correctly, Say was in his time when we met in the 1820s. I have since heard that he travels as I do."

"I don't want to flatter myself, but did you come to Seattle to visit me?"

"I hate to disappoint you, but I do not set my own itinerary. These trips just happen, and end as abruptly. So you should finish asking your questions as soon as possible."

This caused my head to spin. I tried to recall where we were in our conversation and what other topics I should explore.

"Well." I tried to collect my thoughts. "You were going to tell me about your experiences with the Mississippi Company. Let's start with John Law. Explain what his plan was."

"John Law was a Scottish banker working in Paris when I was there. He was about ten years older than me, and more of a politician than a banker. He was charismatic and social with the ladies and less interested in the ways of business. But he was a human abacus—he made his first fortune counting cards at the gambling tables of the wealthy in Paris. He attracted the wealthy since they all wanted to best him at cards, but as far as I know it never happened, unless he wanted it to. Around the gambling tables he met all the most influential people in France.

"Your ideas, Peter, about economics, seem fairly radical to me, but you could not hold a candle to John. His ideas turned French economics upside down, and eventually did the same thing to the country. He expounded on his ideas about money to whomever he could find. Unlike you and me, he thought of money as wealth. He believed a country could convert its land possessions into money without going through the work of creating a wealth making mechanism. His downfall occurred when he convinced the public to exchange their gold and silver for paper notes with trading rights to one particular French territory in the Mississippi delta.

"He believed he could acquire wealth in the delta and load it on a fleet of ships and bring it back to France. His delusion began with a trading monopoly in the Louisiana territory granted by the crown. He neglected the part about the territory needing to have a product to trade for French products. That uncivilized land of swamps and native people had nothing to trade or even steal. There was no wealth to be found there. He put the creation of money, in this case shares, ahead of product making.

"I can only assume John thought that, failing sales, he could plunder the territory. Plunder had been lucrative for the Spanish in Mexico and in the Inca Empire. But John was not so lucky. His land was not endowed with riches. He used the gold and silver of his investors in a futile attempt to generate business when there was none.

"He magnified his difficulties by enticing the French government into a debt swap that made no sense. He traded an agreement to pay off French sovereign debt in exchange for his monopoly trade authority.

"On paper the business seemed viable, especially when you considered the immense wealth the Spanish had extracted from their New World territory. I was initially taken in and invested heavily beside the hopeful."

"Why didn't you investigate it before investing?"

"That was impractical. The location was half way around the world in a corner that had been visited by fewer than 100 Europeans. But I began to look at how the financial side of the scheme worked and quickly became a critic. Do you know much about John Law?"

"I only know that he was the banker responsible for the Mississippi Company bubble. I know nothing of his personal history."

"He came from a wealthy Scottish banking family. He built a life around his obsession with gambling. When he was twenty-three he challenged a rival to a duel over the affections of an attractive woman in London. The duel lasted only a moment, as John with a single parry and thrust ran his sword through his opponent's chest. He was arrested a couple days later and charged with murder at Old Bailey.

"He was unfortunate to be tried by the sadistic hanging judge, Salathiel Lovell. He was convicted of murder and sentenced to death, but the sentence was later reduced to a fine since his offense was not murder, but manslaughter. Outraged, the brother of the slain man appealed and John was incarcerated again, but he escaped from prison and traveled to Amsterdam."

"Fascinating character, but why did you turn against him?"

"Although I agreed with some of his policies, most were not realistic for international trade. It was not his ideas that launched him into the chambers of wealth and power. He benefited a great deal simply from timing.

"France at the time had a failing economy. There was so little actual coinage in the country that business could not function. Coinage was not available to make purchases or pay for goods. The banks just did not have enough gold and silver to fulfill all the needs of the economy. John proposed a solution that required neither gold nor silver. He offered a system of paper money."

"Did he invent paper money?"

"No, but he implemented the largest system in Europe. Louis XIV had spent all the gold and silver in the royal treasury so the options for the government were limited. Eventually, the situation in France became so desperate that the Regent, Philippe d' Orléans, appointed John Law as Controller General of Finances and allowed him to implement his paper money scheme.

"The first step was to create a national bank. In 1716, John Law established the Banque Générale Privée to promote the use of paper money. He would then use that paper money to solve the debt problem of the monarchy with funds from the public obtained through the selling of shares in private ventures such as the Mississippi Company. The King's contribution to the scheme was the grant of monopoly rights to trade in the Mississippi delta.

"Some of the policies John implemented worked well. I liked his focus on increasing the money supply through entrepreneurial ventures. In the two years following this change, industrial activity actually grew by 60%, and in the area of trade where most of the funds were invested, the number of ships carrying French goods grew from 16 to 300. But like most gamblers he did not know when to quit. He had no restraints. Every venture to John was a winning hand.

"When he formed the Mississippi Company, backed by paper money from Banque Générale Privée, the shell game moved to shaky ground. Although the plan had worked well to pay off French debtors with paper money from this new bank, trading in foreign waters required hard currency and the bank had little. So long as trade was primarily a barter arrangement, everything worked according to John's analysis. French goods could be exchanged for sugar and cotton from the Americas and no hard currency was required, or so he supposed. Unfortunately, he overlooked a fundamental problem for his company. The Mississippi Company had nothing to trade and the land that backed the stock had no value since the colony produced little. The people who purchased shares found they owned a piece of a company that did not make money."

"So, what guillotined paper money," I said, "wasn't the paper money promise at the front end of the transaction, but that the expenditure did not pay off in a profit. John Law was fine buying ships and hiring sailors to traverse the Atlantic. His error was a business error. There were no products to load on his ships in New Orleans and carry back to Paris and sell for a profit. The concept of paper money was not wrong. It was John Law's use of the money on ventures without a profitable outcome that caused the Mississippi Company to collapse. Is that correct?"

"Yes. I have to admit I was an early player and allowed many people to use my bank's resources to invest. The investment wave that John Law started created a momentum that many investors after me followed to their great disappointment when they discovered the Company could not produce profits.

"I had more foresight than my fellow investors and sold my shares before the collapse became an avalanche. Those who did not sell suffered immense losses and this included John who believed his own propaganda. It is better to know the basics than to be clever and flamboyant, and forget the fundamental. That is the story of the Mississippi Company and John Law."

I stood up, tired from sitting in the metal chairs. I turned around and looked down into the water. Richard stood up and joined me. I asked, "What is the lesson mankind should take from that experience?"

Richard looked down and stared at the stainless steel water spouts refilling the shallow pond. "The problem was not John Law's innovative ideas; he simply had too much power. He was able to implement ideas that were marginal or had not been tested. The result was a mix of good and bad. The bad apples spoiled all the good. If his power had been curtailed or limited to some degree the final result would not have been so catastrophic for France.

"The country never recovered. With all the benefits of weather, geography, infrastructure, culture, beautiful people, and cleverness, France struggled to achieve the wealth of England.

"This ingrained pattern of financial crisis followed by political insecurity has kept the country well below its economic potential. France to a certain extent has ignored economics and concentrated on the other sciences of human behavior. A country cannot ignore the hard work of building businesses and concentrate solely on building civic facilities. England took the other path and that is the difference between the two countries."

"The legacy of John Law persists today in the idea that government can create as much money as it wants without significant consequences," I said. "Do you think the French—"

There was a cacophonous squeal, and a torrent of police vehicles, an explosion of pulsating, swirling red and blue lights, roiled down the steep hills of Seattle. From the far end of 2nd Avenue a panicked black Camaro emerged, dodging buses and cars as it headed toward us.

Investment

Richard's head jerked around to face the approaching vehicle, his eyes wide with fear. As the Camaro approached, Richard wrapped his arms over the top of his head in an attempt to muffle the sound of the crash. He staggered backward toward me.

In the next instant the Camaro flipped onto its roof and slid past us, spinning down the street. Pedestrians screamed. Onlookers gathered at windows and strained to see a piece of the action. Richard and I stood our ground, stunned by the noise and the chaos surrounding us.

The Camaro came to a stop in the middle of the street, still spinning on its roof. The police conclave arrived immediately after and encircled the now smoldering wreck.

The police car doors swung open in unison. Officers slid from their seats, drew their guns, and took up positions behind their car doors.

Three of the officers slowly stepped out from behind their protection with guns pointed at the black Camaro. They walked cautiously toward the vehicle, stopping and crouching every couple of steps to peer through its broken windows.

There was no motion inside the car. There was no sound from the sidewalks. In silence one officer moved up to the passenger window, pointed his pistol in every corner of the car, then moved closer and looked inside. He shouted at the driver trapped in a seat belt trapeze below the steering wheel. "DON'T MOVE! DON'T MOVE!" The shout reverberated in the glass-walled canyons. There was no response. He shouted again and again: "DON'T MOVE! DON'T MOVE!" There was no response.

Two other officers approached the driver's door. After a couple of shouts, one of them holstered his weapon, reached in, and grabbed the driver, still clinging to the steering wheel. The officer pulled at the driver and he fell out of his seat belt into a lump on the ceiling of the car. The officer quickly checked the man for a pulse and then pulled him through the window onto the street.

Richard spoke: "Was that an arrest?"

"I think that was the plan, but the driver obviously resisted."

"Is he dead?"

"Yeah, it looks that way to me. It is a telling sign when the police pull you out on the ground and then just stand over you and talk.

"The police may want a statement from us. Let's go back to the pool and wait to see if they want any information from us."

"Do you want to finish your question?"

"Let's see. Oh yeah, do you think the French took the path toward economic stagnation knowingly or accidentally?"

"France is the same as every other country. No country has systems in place to guide its growth. The English were lucky and the French less so, but as John Law knew, but ignored, the dice are fickle."

Richard looked down into the pond as we approached and noticed all the coinage at the bottom. I noticed the bewilderment in his eyes, and said, "People throw coins into a pool nowadays to bring them good luck, and then on some dark winter night the pond is emptied and the coins are collected and given to charity. The pond is filled again in the spring."

Richard nodded his head. "I owe you a lesson about the Mississippi bubble that you can use to help your country prevent a similar situation occurring. My advice is too late for your recent bubble experience, but there will be another soon. Bubbles are just like playing at a craps table. When you place a bet, or make an investment that increases in value, you are faced with the question: should you let it ride or take your winnings? This question will never go away as long as investment has risk.

"My answer to the question is: more education. Learn as much as you can about investment and dice games, and you will be able to cut your losses. People accuse me of wrongdoing in the Mississippi Company, but the truth is that I was just the most educated player. Isn't that the player who should win?"

"Yes. That sounds right. Thank you for that explanation. It is great to hear the facts from someone who was there. You were also involved in the South Sea Bubble. Was that the same thing?"

"Yes, the South Sea Company was the English version of the Mississippi Company. They both developed as attempts to solve the financial problems of a national government, and as a way for a few rich men to get richer through finance. In both cases government created a company to use new money-making stratagems developed in the business sector. In neither case did it work.

"We can look back and describe these efforts as financial trickery, but at the time those people had no idea what an economic system was or how one worked. Remember, I was the first person to a write a book explaining how the economic system functioned, and my book was not finished until after both bubbles had collapsed.

"Those bubbles were not planned. They were frauds by money-hungry people, mostly government officials who had no idea what they were playing with. These were not experienced entrepreneurs expanding their businesses. These were strivers who saw the success of some very clever businesspeople and wanted to emulate it. The promoters of both of these schemes were government officials; neither was hatched in someone's barn. Both companies were chartered by national governments and approved by the legislature or the monarchy. In the case of the South Sea Company, a King or Queen acted as Manager during most of the company's existence."

I nodded in agreement. "In our most recent financial bubble, the housing crisis, the irony is that the government blames the banking sector although it had regulators inside the banks overseeing every action. It is like the government funding a voyage of discovery, sending their navy to protect the fleet, and then claiming innocence when overrun by pirates."

A police officer appeared behind me. "Did you gentlemen see what happened?" I jumped three feet sideways, imagining imminent arrest. In my peripheral vision, I noticed Richard was as white as a ghost and paralyzed from head to foot.

I quickly recovered and turned to the officer. "We heard the crash and watched the car flip over, but that's about it."

"Did you see why the car flipped over?"

"I didn't. Did you, Richard?"

"No."

"Did you hear any gunshots?"

"I didn't. How about you, Richard?"

"No."

"Okay, then. Can you write your names and phone numbers at the bottom of this form?"

"Sure, but my friend here does not have a number in the U.S."

"Can you get in touch with him?"

"Yeah, sure."

"Okay, then just put your phone number after his name."

I filled out the sheet and handed it back to the officer.

"Thanks. You two are free to go."

We watched the officer walk up the street and talk to people on the sidewalk until he disappeared from view.

"Were those short rifles your police used? I could not see a flintlock on their weapons."

"We call them guns, but the principle is the same. They shoot a bullet."

"In my time the police used a bow and arrow. I remember one time I arrived with my lawyer for a meeting only to have my carriage surrounded by a dozen police officers pointing arrows at me."

"That must've been frightening."

"Especially since the police corps had spent the preceding four hours drinking in an adjacent pub."

"Drunk police with weapons drawn–that is a frightening picture. What caused the police to surround your carriage?"

"It was some trumped up charge by a disgruntled South Sea investor who wanted to use the Magistrate's power to prevent me from collecting on his debts. I was arrested and thrown in jail for a few hours until my lawyer could speak to the Magistrate.

"Fortunately, in this case I was traveling with my lawyer. That did not stop the crowds from gathering around my coach and accompanying us to the courthouse shouting obscenities. At one point my lawyer climbed onto the roof of the coach to explain the situation and throw a few coins, which cleared a path for our coach to move. That was really all the crowd wanted. Justice was not their concern.

"That reminds me that you asked about a lesson from my life for you to apply in today's financial world.

"In terms of lessons to be learned, the South Sea Company is an encyclopedia of financial mistakes. Its flawed execution illustrates that a company managed by government is prone to failure due to the bureaucratic nature of the supervisory system, and the political tendency to grant special favors. But, to put all this in context, it is important to understand the extent of the financial system in the early 18th century.

"When people earned profits they kept that money in banks because banks provided safety. Banks did not pay interest on deposits. People did not convert their bank accounts to coinage because transporting bags of gold and silver coins was unsafe. Remember, Peter, paper money did not exist. Robbery was the main concern of wealthy depositors. That is why they used banks.

"Banks made their profits providing safety and security for currency deposits. For most merchants, this security was a sufficient reason to keep their money in a bank. They did not concern themselves with earning a return on their deposits since there were few opportunities to do so.

"The only opportunity to earn interest income was to purchase government bonds that paid a small interest. Although wealthy merchants often formed consortiums in order to fund large commercial efforts like ship building or trading ventures, this was not an option for a small or medium sized business."

"It sounds like business opportunities were severely restrained. Did government consider business a significant driver of the economy or more of a nuisance?"

"Government had no concept of an economy as a system that creates jobs and income. The only interest government had in business was as a source of tax revenue. Government did not recognize their responsibility to invigorate the economy with wealth making opportunities. That is why there were so few investment opportunities for business, or any citizen for that matter.

"Investing in land was another marginal opportunity, but that was complicated by a class of owners unwilling to part with what was usually an inheritance. Then the state stepped in with its regulations, further frustrating land transfers. Against this backdrop, an investment opportunity like the South Sea Company was very attractive. The company offered a way to exchange illiquid government holdings for highly liquid shares. The investment seemed safe since the underlying security was still a government bond, and in addition, people got the potential upside of part-ownership in a business with monopoly trading rights in a part of the developing colonies of the Americas."

"I must ask the obvious questions: how did the South Sea Company actually work, and why did the government participate?"

"The structure was very simple. People purchased shares from the Company that paid an annual dividend. The Company took the money from the share sale and purchased government debt so that it would have a reliable source of income to make dividend payments. The government liked the deal because the Company paid more than the going rate for its debt, and the Company simplified the process for the government by having a single debt holder to pay. Of course, the real reason the South Sea Company secured the approval of the Parliament was a series of arrangements for discounted shares to be sold to the leadership of the legislative chambers. As in most government activities corruption reared its ugly head."

"So the South Sea Company was created to enable a group of corrupt politicians to make money?"

"That is essentially correct, but the plan didn't work because, like the Mississippi Company, the business side of the equation did not work. When the bubble ultimately collapsed, Parliament launched an investigation that concluded with the impeachment of Ministers Lord Stanhope and Lord Sunderland, the Postmaster General and the Southern Secretary, and the imprisonment of the Chancellor of the Exchequer. Since most of these individuals were given their shares, they did not suffer financial losses as acutely as the small business owners and merchants who often borrowed to purchase their shares. These people went bankrupt and caused extreme financial harm to the bankers and goldsmiths who had lent them money. The public exercised its outrage against their local bankers. Many people suggested that bankers be put into sacks full of snakes and dropped into the murky Thames. The politicians escaped the public's wrath."

"Didn't the bankers deserve such scorn?"

"Things would have been much better if people had listened to their bankers and exercised more caution. I was one of those bankers and had many clients who refused to listen to my recommendation to not purchase shares. I explained to Lady Mary Herbert, daughter of the Earl of Pembroke, that many savvy investors expected to exit before the inevitable collapse, and she should not try to compete with them. She did not listen and she lost a fortune but still blamed me. The lesson is to engage a financial advisor and follow his advice. I cannot blame the bankers since their job was to enable their clients to make investments; investment advice, if sought at all, was of secondary importance. Their clients made their own choices."

"What other lessons can we learn from this event?"

"One unfortunate lesson is that government cannot run a business. I say unfortunate because so many people think government can do anything and readily place their future in the hands of the government. Power is a poor substitute for expertise. What the investors in the South Sea Company learned is that politicians are suited to cajole people into investments, but their lack of knowledge of the business arts makes them a costly business partner.

"Business requires special skills and experience. The South Sea Company example shows those skills are not found in political leaders. The government managers were unable to control Company costs. They were unable to find profitable endeavors. They lost money on the kinds of ventures that normal businesspeople with far fewer resources found success in. They failed at the slave trade, at simple goods trading, and even at whaling. Not because the economic situation was different for them, but because they made the simplest of business mistakes. As whalers they were unable to hire experienced sailors, as slave traders they failed to get the proper permits and had to sell their slaves at a loss, and as simple traders they delivered goods for which there was no market. They sent a ship to South America in an area near the equator with a load of woolen goods!"

"I can see where the skills of politics may differ greatly from those required to be a successful entrepreneur. Are there any lessons that a budding entrepreneur could find helpful? Or lessons that would apply to any business endeavor?"

"One simple lesson is to look under the covers. Many people were persuaded to invest, because they believed the potential cash flow was huge. The problem was that achieving this potential required Spain to forego a return on the colonies that they discovered and developed. Any reasonable analysis would have revealed that this was highly unlikely. The lesson to learn is to evaluate a business opportunity based on foreseeable cash flow and ignore potential cash flows until they actually start to dribble in.

"The general lesson is to carefully evaluate every investment before listening to the marketing pitch. And after listening to the marketing pitch, carefully extract all the exaggerations and ignore them.

"The lesson for legislatures, and for every citizen, is to realize that although there are many advantages to government borrowing, in the end it is always burdensome and harmful to the people. Moderation in spending and taxation is best."

"What about borrowing by individuals and companies? Should that be encouraged or discouraged?"

"The system of borrowing and lending is what drives the economy. More is always better for those groups that will earn more and expand the economy. There is a direct relationship between business borrowing and wealth expansion, but for the state there is no connection. The state depends on taxes from these same groups to repay its extravagance. The citizenry may not have the capacity or desire to work to repay the state's debt.

"That is my story about financial bubbles, tell me yours. Standing here below this symbol of financial extravagance tell me about your housing crisis and the disappearance of this once great banking institution."

"As in your tale about the South Sea Company, many people felt the bankers who occupied this building deserved to be put into bags with snakes. Also, like your tale, this is a story of the government using the banking system for their own benefit. Unlike your tale, the government officials here escaped punishment because they ran the investigation."

Richard asked, "What was the government official's motivation?"

"In our country the electorate is broken into two groups represented by two political parties. One party, the Democrats, represents the interests of people who earn minimal income. The Democrats often seek benefits for this group. Housing is a popular item on their list. Ten years before the housing bubble they passed legislation requiring banks to make new house loans to this group of low income people. Making these loans was necessary for banks to qualify for making other more lucrative loans. Each year the number of low income loans required to qualify for higher margin loans increased.

Eventually, the group that qualified for these loans was so deficient in income that the banks went too far in offering creative loan products.

Richard asked, "Why did the banks make such distorted loan contracts?"

I replied, "Government regulators required a certain quantity of low income loans and eventually the only way to achieve such quantities required highly complex loan products. The banks complied with the regulators dictums, but eventually their borrowers were simply unable to make the payments and the structure failed."

"So the politicians collapsed the economy trying to ensure their reelection. I can see why they did not come to that conclusion in their investigation!"

"They didn't even come close to that conclusion."

"That is very similar to the failure of the Mississippi Company," Richard noted. "The simple lesson is that the state should not force business to work where the economics are flawed, no matter how attractive the opportunity or socially appealing the outcome. In those situations the state needs to step in with its own money.

"Business, like crops, will only flourish where conditions are favorable. May I assume that many of the people in this building lost their jobs because a politician exploited a flaw in the social system to guarantee his reelection? That sets a bad precedent for the impoverished and the unemployed. Looking at this magnificent building reminds me that many years are needed to increase abundance to such a high level, but only months are needed to destroy abundance by changing the conditions of wealth creation."

"Richard, thank you for taking the time to explain the circumstances of both of the famous financial bubbles that occurred during your time as a banker. And now I am running out of time. I must head down to the ferry terminal to catch a boat back to Bainbridge Island."

"Will you take me back to the Merchant Café?"

"Sure, no problem."

"My ghost family will be returning soon."

"Your ghost family! What is that?"

Richard bent back at the waist, feigning a big belly laugh. "I was only spinning your head!"

"Thanks for the exercise!"

Peter, start your memory engine! It will be easy to associate the car wreck with the financial crashes of the Mississippi Bubble and the South Sea Bubble. Both were caused by bad driving by government officials trying to promote either a personal agenda or a political agenda.

Objects of Speculation

The police were finishing their investigation and reopening the street. They completed removing the barricades they had erected to block the northbound lanes of 2nd Avenue. A flood of buses stopped by the car accident now flowed through the intersection and into the transit stop in front of us. Passengers held captive on the buses for more than an hour while police gained control of the accident site poured out onto the sidewalk.

I directed Richard to move south. We merged into the scurrying crowd disembarking from the bus convoy. Twisting and turning, we headed toward the intersection. It was futile. I lifted my arm above the crowd, waved to get Richard's attention, and pointed at the sculpture court. "We can't make it through this obstacle course. Let's wait until the horde dissipates."

We sat back down at one of the metal tables. Richard asked, "Do you want me to answer your last question?"

"About your ghost family?"

"'Family' is not quite correct. My entire family perished in the fire when my house in London burned. These people are my substitute family, acquaintances and friends that I have adopted."

"Can I meet them?"

Richard hesitated. "I must get their permission and see if they really want to meet you."

"Are you meeting anyone important?"

"All my friends are important; do you mean are there any economists among my friends?" Richard asked mischievously.

"Sorry to be so transparent, but I've enjoyed our conversation so much I just got excited about the possibility of meeting another famous economist. Forgive me my nearsightedness. I know the world is full of intriguing people and I would enjoy meeting any of your friends."

"You may get that chance, but first help me get back to the Merchant Café by 5 p.m."

"No problem, Richard. It is only a little after 3 p.m. That gives you plenty of time. The Café is only a twenty minute walk from here."

"Oh, good, then show me some more of your city."

We had been sitting for quite a while and the bus rush was subsiding. "The crowd is diminishing let's resume our stroll down the hill to the waterfront. That's in the direction of my ferry and the Merchant Café."

"Good plan. What way do we go?"

I pointed to the crosswalk on 2nd Avenue. We both walked across.

"Why do you want to get back to the Café by 5? Are you meeting your extended family?"

"Hopefully. I invited them to join me. I expect them to arrive sometime after 5, but they could arrive late tonight. Ghosts are not noted for their punctuality or reliability," Richard said in a jaunty manner.

A food truck passed by, headed down the hill. "What was that? It looked like a metal pig!" Richard shrieked with the delight of a six year old.

It was one of Seattle's most iconic food trucks, a restaurant on ten wheels called Minimus/Maximus, because they serve a sweet sauce (Minimus) and a spicy sauce (Maximus) on their most popular menu item, a pulled pork sandwich. It's not the menu that makes the food truck iconic, but the stainless steel exterior shaped like a pig. The truck's grill is sculpted to look like a gigantic pig snout. Above the nose, a cool pair of sunglasses covers the windshield to give the pig some panache. Sticking up above the cab is a prominent pair of pig's ears. The remainder of the pig's physique is perfectly crafted into an Airstream-shaped stainless steel chassis.

Smiling at the absurdity of trying to explain this phenomenon to Richard, I said, "Remember what I told you about cars when we were at the Columbia Center? This is a type of car, only bigger, that we call a truck. A truck in England is called a lorry."

"Oh, I know what a lorry is," Richard exclaimed.

"The shape of the truck is a promotional device to attract customers. The truck is a restaurant that sells pork sandwiches. The restaurant owner thought designing the truck to look like a pig would attract the curious when the truck is parked and open for business."

"Let's go and stop it and get a pork sandwich," Richard chortled.

"I think they are finished for the day and are going back to their home restaurant to park."

"What was that pig made of?"

"It's a type of stainless steel similar to the cladding on the steel columns we were looking at outside the bank."

"It is a regal looking material. Does it last as long as marble?"

"That is difficult to say precisely, since both marble and steel are extremely long lived materials. The main difference is the physical properties of the material. Marble is made of sand particles pressed tightly together and steel is a combination of iron ore and coking coal melted together. The main difference in these materials is the strength of the finished product in terms of weight. It takes far less steel to support the weight of a building than it would marble. Also steel has much greater bridging strength which we call shear strength. You can bridge a small stream with a horizontal girder of steel, but a stone bridge would require an arch.

"Advances in the manufacturing process of steel reduced the cost of production. Steel became competitive with wood and stone. That allowed increases in production and variety of output giving an immense push to economic growth in the city. It turned a horizontal cityscape into a forest of skyscrapers multiplying the value of the land many times over. Seventy stories of rental space is 35 times more valuable than 2 stories.

"This discussion gives me an idea. Let's go down to the waterfront and I will show you an amazing steel structure."

"Your citizenry really likes to build things."

"It is our wealth. Most of these buildings are occupied by tenants who pay rent. Am I correct to say that by your definition of wealth these buildings are wealth?"

"Wealth is an object that earns a fee year after year. It is usually land, like a 100-acre farm, but a building that earns rent works the same way. Money can be wealth if used to purchase an interest earning note, but usually money is simply a way of holding value until conversion into a wealth asset or a product you want to consume."

"So you are saying money is not wealth. I understand that, but what about a car?"

"What do you mean?"

"I am sorry. Let me explain the financial situation for a car. Family cars mostly are used to get to work and for shopping. Although the car also is used for recreation we can ignore that aspect for a simple understanding of the financial cost. Let's say my car will last ten years and it costs $36,000, or $3600 annually. Does this cost make me wealthier?"

"What alternatives to a car are there?"

I explained that in a city a person could take the bus for most purposes, rent a car when really needed, and avoid purchasing a car with only some sacrifice of convenience.

Richard said, "It sounds as if a city person might only need to rent a car a couple of times a month. I would subtract the rental costs from the purchase costs and conclude a car is an expense and not wealth."

"What if you sold the car and pocketed the cash?"

Richard drolly responded, "It is still not wealth. It is only money looking for a home."

"Let's try a different item. How does a large quantity of food factor into your idea of wealth? Is enough food to last a year an asset?"

"That is too easy! Food is what enables a person to have enough energy to work 12 hours a day. Without food your most important asset, you, would not work and earn. Think of it this way: it is like oil in a lamp. The lamp has no value without oil to burn. A person is not an asset without the fuel he needs to sustain life. Many wealth-generating assets require fuel, space, food stocks, or supplies to complete the wealth cycle. A printing press is useless without paper, a waterwheel is useless without a grinding stone, and a grinding stone is useless without grain."

"I understand that, but many people consider jewelry or precious stones to be wealth. Are they?"

"Precious stones, gold, art, ceramics, and silks are all in the same class. They are not wealth per se, but objects you can buy with money instead of wealth. They are really adult toys. They are objects of decoration, status, or amusement. None are likely to generate an annual revenue stream. On the other hand, they may appreciate in value, but that makes them objects of speculation. Since I am in the business of speculation I know that, if done properly, speculation can make you very rich. But that does not mean that objects of speculation such as gold and jewels are wealth. It is the timing skill of the speculator that is the wealth in that process."

"It is hard to imagine that gold and jewels are not wealth."

"I did not say they were not valuable, only that they are not wealth. Gold and jewels may be owned almost universally by wealthy people, but the money to purchase their gems likely came not from the gold and jewels they owned, but from their ships that transported corn and wool."

"Why is this distinction important?"

"Seeking wealth is what makes a family secure. It is the same for a country. Now a country that seeks gold and jewels might think itself secure, but if it had no farmland to feed its people it would be in desperate straits. How many jewels would a family give up to feed their starving children?

"The country that helps its entrepreneurs, allows the construction of manufacturing plants, and encourages the development of farmland, and avoids the excessive regulation of natural resource development will fare far better than those that raise impediments to business expansion."

This gave me an idea. "Richard, I want to show you another piece of sculpture. This one is located outside the Seattle Art Museum. Let's go back up this way." I gestured to Richard to turn around and pointed him toward the museum. When he didn't turn I put my hand on his shoulder to turn him. I was slightly shocked to not feel much substance or weight inside his coat as I directed him back up 2nd Avenue. I stored that observation in my mental database for evaluation later.

The Worker

"Richard, I want you to see this famous sculpture because it honors 'the worker in all of us from the village craftsman to the coal miner.' This is not a sculpture unique to Seattle. The tallest version of it is in Frankfurt, Germany. There are numerous copies throughout the United States, including most of the major cities: New York, Los Angeles, Dallas, Minneapolis, and our capitol, Washington D.C. There is even a copy close to China in Seoul, South Korea."

"Do you have a sculpture that honors the entrepreneur?"

"As far as I know we do not, which is somewhat ironic since Seattle is best known for being the home of many of the world's most famous entrepreneurs, such as William Boeing, William Pigott, Bill Gates, Paul Allen, Jeff Bezos, and of course Howard Schultz."

"You should, because entrepreneurs create jobs. Laboring at a job is important, but it all begins with a person who has the vision to see a need that can be filled with a new product."

We reached the intersection across from the Art Museum. "Here we are. See the tall silhouette of a man on the other side of the street? The sculpture was created by Jonathan Borofsky from Maine. It is made of steel, like the column sculpture we looked at earlier. This steel is painted black. The sculpture weighs 20,000 pounds and is 48 feet tall. The piece is called the 'Hammering Man' for obvious reasons, as you will see in a moment. Let's walk down closer."

"It could be an ode to William Shakespeare's line, 'what a piece of work is man'. Very unusual and very tall, but I like it," Richard said, smiling broadly.

We walked down the slight hill on University St. and then crossed over to stand below the sculpture. "You will enjoy this symbolism, Richard. The 'Hammering Man' works from 7 a.m. to 8 p.m. every day except Labor Day. Labor Day is a holiday we celebrate to honor the worker."

"Impressive, but to be truly inclusive I think the city needs to add a sculpture to honor the entrepreneur and the banker who work 16 hours a day."

Looking around to see if he was overheard, I said, "The entrepreneur and especially the banker are not highly regarded. You bear some of the responsibility for the bad reputation of the banker."

Richard pulled back from me. "How is that?"

Looking him in the eye I replied, "Well, you became very rich when the Mississippi Company and South Sea Company appreciated, but the average investor lost money. People do not see that as fair. And bankers have repeated that pattern over the last 300 years."

"That is an inaccurate characterization! Some bankers made money and some bankers lost money. Those who made money were more skilled in the speculation game. Like every game there are winners and losers. You cannot select only the winning players for criticism and sympathize with the losers. Everyone playing the game strove to be a winner. If you criticize any group it should be those who created the game, not the players.

"Your city chooses winners and losers. Is that more fair than letting the contest determine the winners and losers? You select a group of people out of the economy to honor, but ignore the creative businessperson. Where is your monument to Howard Schultz and the people like him who live here? If you follow a path of deciding whom to praise, you will eventually make a mistake. If you are like the French of my time, you will build magnificent palaces of education to honor educators who have never created a single job. Or build monuments to kings who only spend their citizen's money on their personal needs. I admire people who create wealth, not those who take wealth by the size and force of their army or group of bullies."

"I agree with you. I am sure most of my fellow citizens do as well," I said to calm and temper Richard's criticism. "We are not totally under the sway of powerful groups. We honor individual accomplishment. We just want each person to have the means to provide for their own sustenance. I know this is one of your basic ideas: that an individual's income must be sufficient to provide for their economic needs."

"Peter, that is correct. The economy should provide jobs with sufficient income for people to provide for their own basic wants. If an economy cannot provide that level of income, the remainder of the system might grind to a halt. There must be enough economic push to keep the millstones turning."

"That's a principle my country was founded upon. We overthrew the British monarchy because they tried to take away our livelihood with excessive taxation. The revolution led to the establishment of a democratic government with the purpose of liberty and economic freedom. Do you know that the French monarchy was also overthrown?"

"The palace of Versailles is no more?" Richard exclaimed.

"The palace is still there, but the King, Queen, and Court are gone. The building and grounds are now a tourist destination. Recall the story of Marco Polo, when he went to Asia to visit the palaces of the Chinese sovereigns? Now the Chinese come to France to view the fabulous palaces of the French monarchy."

"*Sacre bleu*. Is France now a democracy?"

"Yes, but not a very good one. The government taxes the citizens excessively. Wealthy people are leaving the country and it is difficult to support a family with a small business income. Farmers are in perpetual conflict with taxing authorities. Federal employee unions are huge."

Smiling, Richard said, "It is good to hear some things have not changed."

Enjoying the first warmth of the afternoon, I moved to the sidewalk along First Avenue and suggested to Richard that we go look at another Seattle tourist magnet. I directed him down University Street to where the street ends and the sidewalk turns into a long continuous stairway to the waterfront. When we reached the broad sidewalk along the harbor we walked south toward the ferry terminal.

"I want to show you another type of steel structure. See that white arch above the buildings over there?" I said, pointing to Seattle's Great Wheel.

"Oh my, what is that?"

"That is called a Ferris wheel, named after the man who created the first steel wheel of its kind at the 1893 Exposition in Chicago. It has enclosed seats for people to ride around from bottom to top and back. When we get around this building you will be able to see how it works. This is another use of steel, like the columns and beams that hold up all the tall buildings around here."

"How tall is the wheel?"

"If I recall correctly, it is 175 feet high."

Richard surprised me when he said, "I have ridden in something similar in Asia. It was called a 'Pleasure Wheel' and was operated by six strong men."

"What part of Asia?"

"When I was in Venice I took a ship to see the land on the other side of the Adriatic."

"What was the wheel made of?"

"It was made of wood like a wagon wheel. I suppose it was about twenty feet high, with four seats. When you sat down the men pulled on the spokes, the wheel turned, and you rose to the height of the rooftops. You could see the whole town. It was very popular. People came from far away for a ride."

"Well, Richard, it sounds like your wheel and ours are quite similar. Do you want to take a ride and experience the improvements made in the last 300 years?"

"I would enjoy that."

Richard followed me down the wharf along a warehouse from the 19th century, now converted to retail space selling Seattle knick-knacks. "Now that we are up close, can you figure out how it is held up?"

"No, it looks like magic to me."

"See, the pair of tall pipes on either side support the wheel. The wheel itself hangs off an axle connecting those pair of legs to a pair of wheels separated by about ten feet. All the support members painted white are made of steel. This type of tourist structure dates back to a famous iron monument built in Paris in 1889 for the World's Fair."

"*Magnifico*, a World's Fair in Paris, an appropriate honor bestowed on a worthy city," Richard gushed.

"That monument still exists and is named the Eiffel Tower after the engineer and promoter, Gustave Eiffel, who financed and built it. The tower was constructed to commemorate the overthrow of Louis XVI and the French monarchy in 1798, and the establishment of the democratic French Republic."

"I am not surprised that happened," said Richard. "There was a push in that direction early in the 18th century. The extravagance and focus of the government on pleasure palaces was sure to eventually cause a backlash."

We reached the end of the pier underneath the Great Wheel. At the booth I purchased two $13 tickets. Richard looked up at the network of steel members above us and stood entranced. I directed my dumbstruck companion into the line for loading. "That network of pipes is all made of steel and supports the two wheels and glass cabins."

Not a word out of Richard. I continued, "The glass cabins are called gondolas."

Richard was still in a trance, his neck craned upwards. I nudged him along the loading ramp. The attendants had just stopped the wheel and were unloading passengers from the other side of the gondola cars. Our turn was coming up. "Richard, pay attention to the attendants. They will show you how to load."

Richard came out of his personal fog and focused on the attendants at the top of the loading stair. Soon they signaled us to follow them. "Watch your step. You can sit on either side and change your seat when the gondola is moving. The wheel will make three rotations and then we will stop to load more passengers. We will do that four times." In robotic unison the attendants all said, "Enjoy your ride!"

Richard stepped across the threshold first and took a seat facing the city. I stepped in and sat opposite him, facing Puget Sound, the Olympic Mountains, and my island home, Bainbridge Island. We were the last car to load so we began moving almost immediately. As we took off the gondola swung slightly. Richard startled and tightened his grip on his seat.

"Is this anything like the wheel you rode in the Balkans?" I asked playfully.

"The idea is the same, but not the scale."

As we ascended Richard stiffened. "Are you all right?" I said. "This is very safe. The wheel is only a year old and has been ridden many times without incident." I said reaching for the water bottle in my backpack. "Here, take a drink of water. It will make you feel better."

Richard grabbed the bottle. He took a quick gulp and handed it back. We reached the top in about a minute, and as we descended the green color in his face faded. His insecurity disappeared and was replaced with a slight reddish tint in his cheeks. Since he was stabilizing, I decided to describe the sights to take his attention away from his fears. I turned slightly to look at the view Richard was concentrating on.

"See that tall white tower in the distance? It is called the Space Needle and is the symbol of the city. As citizens of Seattle we like to think of ourselves as being at the forefront of new ideas and leading the world with innovative thinking and designs."

As the gondola started the second climb to the top I could see Richard breathing more regularly and starting to look around, but he didn't speak a word.

"Richard, what do you think?"

His lips tensed like he was getting ready to speak, but nothing came out. The gondola had passed the top and begun to descend when he finally said, "This is a new experience for me. I am not sure I like it."

"Give it some time, Richard, it is an acquired taste. Turn around and look at Puget Sound and the ships heading to China and Japan." I pointed off in the distance to a thin strip of greenery clinging to the horizon. "That is Bainbridge Island where I have a house and family. See how far I have to travel to go to work every day! That large white vessel is one of the ferries I use to travel between my house and the city. Oh, look down there. Do you see that large ship with lettering that reads 'Hyundai'? That is a container ship headed to Asia. The ship is probably carrying electronic devices from Microsoft or aircraft parts from Boeing. How many ships ply the Thames?"

"In my time it took many more ships because they were small. The Thames is just a river, not at all like this immense sound," Richard slowly answered.

I decided to give him a rest, and let him try to relax and enjoy the ride. "Richard, sit back and enjoy the beauty of the day. It looks like the fog is breaking. It will clear rapidly and the black water and gray sky will soon turn bright blue. If you have any questions, just ask."

"I do not have a question, but I have a statement about the flow of money that I want you to include in your book about Cantillon Economics." Richard smiled. "Consider the circular motion of the Great Wheel. Monetary flows are also circular. First, a bank makes a loan to an entrepreneur; second, the entrepreneur creates a product; third, the entrepreneur sells his product; fourth, the entrepreneur repays the bank; fifth, the entrepreneur deposits his profit in the bank. This is the money cycle. This is the only way to increase wealth. As this process is repeated the amount of wealth in the economy grows as entrepreneurs expand their businesses and employ more people. Every job is a wealth-making mechanism.

"Mr. Keynes got it wrong. Government spending, even on worker salaries does not create wealth, because the expenditure must be repaid. It does transfer money from government coffers to individual bank accounts. This gives an illusion of wealth creation, but the amount of total wealth is reduced by the increase in principal and interest owed by the taxpayers. The eventual outcome is a reduction in national wealth."

This will be easy to remember using the Great Wheel as a metaphor. The idea is that the economy follows a circular flow slowly increasing wealth as business profits grow.

Steps to Crisis Recovery

Richard was silent for the remainder of the ride, but he was turning and looking left and right by the time we made our last loop and descended. We walked away from the Great Wheel and I began to consider my day with Richard.

As we passed the fire station adjacent to the ferry terminal we were approached by two golfers carrying their bags and clubs. I couldn't help myself; I said, "You guys are a bit off course."

Richard exclaimed, "Are those golf clubs?"

I rushed forward and gave a tit-ta-tat, tit-ta-tat explanation of Richard's roots and his interest in golf to the blank stares of the golfers now stopped on the sidewalk by the wild haired Irishman. Richard completed my conversation by asking if he could see a ball.

"Sure," the first golfer said, bending down to retrieve a ball from a pocket on the side of his bag. "I am sure it is just like the balls you use in Ireland."

Richard, with eyes bigger than a pirate opening a treasure chest, bent his neck directly over the bag, staring down at what might emerge. The golfer pulled a crisp new ball from his bag and handed it to Richard.

"*Joie de vivre*, this is magnificent. Such workmanship and quality. I have never seen anything like it. I played with balls made by the Robertson family in St. Andrews. They were the best in the world at the time, but this is amazing. Can I see a club?"

"Sure," said the golfer, approaching the end of his tolerance for this interruption. He pulled a five iron out of his bag and handed it to Richard.

Running his hands along the smooth shaft and cradling the toe of the club, Richard exclaimed, "Equally amazing! We played with a cleek. The face of the club was not in the same class as this club of yours."

I recovered the club from Richard's possession and handed it back to the golfer. "Thanks a lot, fellas. We need to catch a ferry. Come along, Richard."

Richard followed my command, still red in the face at the excitement of seeing a modern golf club. Looking to calm his excitement I asked, "Can you explain to me the proper role of government in extracting an economy from a financial crisis?"

"The proper approach for government is to avoid debt and grant a tax holiday or rebate. Of course, if the government is already in debt this strategy will not work because it just would increase the burden on the taxpayer. Taxpayers are not stupid. They realize that pushing into the future the day of reckoning will only make the situation worse. Under those circumstances the only fiscally astute thing that can be done is to reduce the cost of government. Some of the ideas floated during my time were ending the employment of government employees and eliminating government functions such as road building and ship building. I hope that explains how government through fiscal restraint can strengthen the confidence of people in the stability of their savings and assets. Peter, does that match with your experience?"

"Well, we certainly recognize that the economy works better when there is economic stability, but it is not a policy goal. We focus on maintaining jobs through government spending to reverse the trend in the private economy. Increased government spending is our basic approach.

"Once savings and assets are not under threat, people will next look at the stability of their job. For most people the stability of their job is the biggest financial risk they face. People realize the security of their job depends upon the vitality of the overall economy. How can the risk of job elimination be reduced?"

Richard said, "This is partially achieved by increasing the security of the monetary system. An extra push comes from the public's positive reception to the fiscal obedience of government that I just described. But a country must go further. A country must create an economic environment conducive to commercial and manufacturing expansion."

As Richard continued, my attention was captured by the angled streaks of sunlight emanating from a dramatic ragged crevasse in the cloud formation on the horizon. Light streamed in arrow-straight lines to strike the edge of the Sound in a pool of sharp white light.

My oblivious companion rattled on. "This is one of the easiest of all economic goals, but the most difficult for governments to accept. It is a policy approach that requires government to trust business people and customer choice. If companies follow the path of doing what is in the best interest of their customers, they are unlikely to breach social standards.

"All government regulation is based on the assumption that companies will not follow that path. Certainly the truth falls somewhere between the two extremes, but government almost always designs its standards and enforcement strategies based on a worst-case scenario. Consequently, government over-reaching is likely to impede business success. This is critically important since business in the best of times is very difficult to sustain and excessive government interference can disrupt a fragile business initiative. In other words, job security depends on a business environment conducive to business success. It is that simple."

That was a lot to take in. I found myself trying to extract a simple understanding. "So if we go back to the analogy of the cart stuck in the mud, you are saying that government is the road builder and the cart operator is the businessman. The government should concentrate on building roads that drain and are surfaced for travel in bad weather. The businessman should purchase carts with large capacity beds to move many goods quickly and safely along the road. If each performs their task competently and consistently no jobs or assets will be at risk, and the cost of goods when they reach the market will be as low as possible. Government will also benefit since they will receive the maximum taxes from sales. Are you saying that, in an economic downturn, look for the pieces of the economy that are broke and precipitated the crisis?"

Richard smiled. "Find out what is broken and fix it."

"We have had two major economic downturns in the past 100 years. The first was in 1929 when the stock market crashed. The second was in 2008 when a housing bubble burst."

Richard sighed. "I am unfortunately an expert in stock speculation and bubbles. Most stock speculation that turns out badly results from uninformed or unreasonable profit expectations. Was that your situation?"

"Not in 1929, but more recently we did have a minor stock collapse called the Internet Bubble that was clearly based on unreasonable profit expectations... Well, just a second, let me reconsider whether the Great Depression in 1929 was based on unreasonable profit expectations. That crisis occurred at the end of a ten year interval after World War I during which the United States supplied most of the agricultural products to Europe as the continent recovered from war. The crisis occurred when our Congress passed high tariffs on the recovering industries in Europe, which prompted retaliatory tariffs by European countries and severely reduced cross-Atlantic trade.

"I am no expert in this topic, but it seems likely there were people who evaluated stocks too optimistically in this declining business environment. There were also some emerging industries like radio that did provide reasonable profit expectations, so excessive speculation was certainly a contributing factor. I still think the biggest problem was a lack of knowledgeable regulation. Banks made far too many loans to speculators."

Richard responded, "We had the same problem in both the Mississippi Company and South Sea Company. People cannot resist the pull of the herd. I do think the government should ensure full and complete disclosure of company assets and profitability. People are just not smart enough to avoid stepping into a hole. Government must require full disclosure. The problem in my time was that government was the primary agent of these companies. That is the worst possible situation. A government promoting a speculative company in which they have an investment position is a recipe for corruption and a financial crisis."

As we approached the stair up to the ferry terminal I asked with genuine curiosity, "In the book I am planning to write about your theories, what would you like me to highlight?"

Richard bent his head forward, looked at the ground, and slowly scratched the back of his neck. "In my time governments had a fundamental misunderstanding of what drives an economy. I would like to correct that misunderstanding." He raised his head and looked directly at me like he expected some protest.

"That is fine with me," I said. "Please just take a moment to clarify what that misunderstanding was?" I raised my arms and showed my empty palms in an unintended submissive sign. Struck by the effect his response made on me, I was concerned how well this discussion might go.

Richard relaxed and spoke in a more conversational tone. "It is the confusion between money and wealth. Government focuses too much effort on trying to get more money. An economy does not prosper when government has lots of money to spend. An economy prospers when people are secure in their possession of a tool or wealth creating mechanism that will make money for them this year, next year, and beyond."

Delighted that Richard had answered my question so thoughtfully, I asked, "What focus does government need to change and how should it do that?"

"First, it wastes effort on controlling the quantity of money in circulation. It is not the amount of money, but the uses money is put to that creates wealth. Money spent to clear land and prepare for planting produces more wealth than money spent on a fine silk jacket. The first expenditure produces a wealth generating mechanism, a farm, and the other a well-dressed woman. Government does not understand that distinction.

"Government should avoid spending for the sake of spending and instead concentrate on how to induce the business sector to produce more wealth creating mechanisms. I do not mean just farms and factories. The main wealth generating mechanism is the entrepreneur. Government does not create jobs, entrepreneurs do."

The sun came out fully now and the air warmed along the sidewalk. Richard unbuttoned his overcoat, took it off, and laid it across his arm, revealing a frilly white shirt clearly from the 18th century. I looked at him like a child confused by a magic trick. I so much wanted him to be real, but I knew I must be being duped by an eccentric from the 21st century. Nevertheless, before the curtain fell I wanted to ask a few more questions. "What do you believe is the foundation of economic theory? Is it supply and demand? Is it how to redistribute goods? Is it how to create jobs? Is it wealth-creating mechanisms? Is it banking? Is it trading? Is it fractional lending? What?"

"Let me quote Shakespeare: 'There are more things in heaven and earth, Horatio, than are dreamt of in your philosophy.' There are so many factors at work that to believe you have found the Philosopher's Stone is ridiculous hubris. Be satisfied with the source of water you have discovered and seek other methods to look younger, but do not kid yourself into believing there is but one formula for a long and successful life."

I was stunned by the wisdom of his statement. "Richard, that is an extraordinary thought with which to end our day. I must go up these stairs and get on my ferry. To get back to the Merchant Café you just follow this sidewalk past the ferry entrance and take the first crosswalk across the street. Go three or four blocks up the hill and you will be at the Merchant Café. Goodbye, and nice meeting you. I hope we meet again."

I could feel the cars moving onto the ferry behind me so I quickly turned and took a couple of steps up the stairs. Richard called my name.

"Peter, do you want to meet Jean Baptiste Say? Be at the Old Towne Pizza restaurant in Portland on October 1st."

I turned back to clarify what Richard had said, and got struck broadside by a man taking two steps at a time. "Sorry," I said.

"Jeez, buddy, just keep going!"

I quickly righted myself and moved to a corner on the stair platform out of the traffic pattern. I looked down on the sidewalk to where Richard had stood a minute before. There was no sign of him. He had disappeared. How could a man in a frilly white shirt vanish? Should I go after him? But where was he? I moved to the railing and leaned out and looked north and south along the sidewalk. There was no sign of him.

There was clearly no way to track him down before my ferry departed. I turned and walked up the stair and into the ferry terminal. I still did not know which Richard Cantillon I met, but I now knew much more about the man. I also knew I would be in

Portland, Oregon on October 1 to meet Jean Baptiste Say.

I walked upstairs to the waiting room and took a seat in a quiet corner. *What happened? What gems did I hear that should go into my new Cantillon book?*

I can explain that Cantillon's view of connecting money creation to product creation requires putting him in the camp opposed to monetary expansion through deficit spending. He really believes monetary expansion needs to be matched with wealth expansion, with the creation of wealth making mechanisms.

He dislikes government disrupting the market through policy and manipulation. This viewpoint anchors his observation about the economic shoreline that the ship of state should avoid. He clearly sees government manipulation of the money supply as an irritant more than an effective economic action. Interest rates and inflation are not as important considerations as product innovation. To add a positive note, I should explain his theory that government should work to improve conditions that support entrepreneurial enterprises.

That is the key to his ideas: disarm the government shore batteries and let the entrepreneurs land without resistance.

I was now surrounded by anxious shipmates, ready to go aboard. I began to slowly slip forward, like the surf sliding off the shore back down into the sea. I didn't resist. I let the motion of the crowd drag me onto the boat.

EPILOGUE

Help me spread the word about New Market Economics. Go to RandMcGreal.com., and read the next book in the series, <u>Killing an Idea</u> about Jean Baptiste Say. The end. I hope you found this journey into economic theory pleasant and informative.

www.ingramcontent.com/pod-product-compliance
Lightning Source LLC
Chambersburg PA
CBHW051501170526
45166CB00001B/338